THE 21ST CENTURY JOB SEARCH

by

Bruce A. Hurwitz, Ph.D.
President
Hurwitz Strategic Staffing, Ltd.

www.hsstaffing.com

This publication is designed to provide accurate and authoritative information regarding the subject matter concerned. The author is not involved in rendering legal, accounting, or other similar professional services. If legal advice or other expert assistance is required, the services of a competent professional should be sought.

Library of Congress Cataloguing-in-Publication Data

Hurwitz, Bruce A.

The 21st Century Job Search / Bruce A. Hurwitz – 1st ed.

ISBN-13: 978-1985101135
ISBN-10: 1985101130

To my former career counseling clients, candidates and students.
I probably learned more from you than you did from me!

Table of Contents

Preface

People seem to believe that entering a new century means that there is a new way to do just about everything, or at least there should be. That's silly. At least as regards conducting an effective job search, the only thing different in this, the second decade of the twenty-first century, from previous centuries, is technology – you can literally find networking events at the push of a button, and apply for hundreds of jobs a week, if you already have a computer and internet access, virtually for free! (Well, there are two other things, but you'll have to read a bit more to find out what they are!) The basics are still the same:

You have to be presentable. You have to be professional. You have to be polite. You have to be a good communicator. And, as always, it is not *what* you know but *who* you know.

A job search is a marathon, not a sprint. During this journey we will be taking together, we will travel through all the phases of a successful job search. I will be blunt. As readers of my LinkedIn articles – on which this book is based, at least in part - know, that's just the way I am. There are things that I have written that people have found offensive. If you want to be treated like a baby, this book is not for you. If you want to read about rainbows, unicorns and mermaids, there are plenty of other books on conducting an effective job search that you may find enjoyable. Whether they will be useful is another matter.

It is not my job to tell you what you *want* to hear. It is my job to tell you what you *need* to hear. And that is what you will find in the following pages.

This book is based on my experiences, since 2003, as an executive recruiter and career counselor. It is not an academic treatise. I know how to write them. Both my Master's thesis and doctoral dissertation were published by leading publishers. In addition, I have scores of articles and reviews that have been published in peer-reviewed journals, not to mention newspapers and magazines, and two previous self-published books. If I wanted to make this academic, I could. So why didn't I?

First, it would have been boring to write and even more boring to read! But, more importantly, getting a job is not an academic or theoretical exercise; it is real life. I take it seriously. I am not involved with what *should be* in a perfect world, but with what *is*. You are going to learn what really happens in a job search, focused on the only person who matters, the employer. That's right; the employer is the one who matters, not you. How's that for being blunt?

Prior to the employer convincing you to accept a job offer, you have to convince them to make the offer. That's why they matter and you don't (at least not until the end of the process).

Before we get started, there is a critical question you must ask yourself: Do you really want a new job, or just new responsibilities? I have had a number of clients come to me saying they wanted new jobs. It turned out that they liked their bosses, their colleagues and their clients. What they really wanted were some new challenges. We came up with plans which they submitted to their bosses. They kept their jobs but changed them. Maybe that is all you need. Think about that before starting a job search.

The most important question for a candidate or an employer concerns "fit." Will the candidate be a good fit? Will they fit into the corporate culture? In addition to technology, another new thing in the 21st Century, for good or evil, is Political Correctness. (When there is a culture of respect, there is no need for Political Correctness, but forget I wrote that because it probably is not politically correct!) If you are PC and they are not, or if you aren't and they are, even if you get the job, it may not last. It just won't be "a good fit." Walking on egg shells, having to think if there is even the remote possibility of offending even a single individual, albeit totally innocently and without malice, may be idiotic but, in some places, it is how things are.

We will get into this in more detail as we progress. But for now I just want you to note that little things can matter and there are a great many complications, figurative landmines, in a job search. My goal in writing this book is to help you avoid stepping on any. It is also to provide you with the tools to differentiate yourself from your competition, by providing you with a real-world inspired guide to writing effective cover letters and résumés, having exemplary questions to ask in interviews, and phenomenal answers to the questions you will be asked. At the end of the day, *being able to positively differentiate yourself from your competition is an imperative if you are going to get a job offer.*

Have a safe, productive and successful journey.

Bruce A. Hurwitz
March, 2018
New Jersey, USA

Part One: Preparing

A job search is art, not science. Everything I will advise you to do is based on actual experience, either my own as an executive recruiter dealing with countless candidates for positions with my employer clients, or my experiences helping career counseling clients travel on their road to career success, be they recent high school or college graduates, individuals looking for their next opportunity, seasoned professionals, retirees not knowing what to do with themselves, or veterans.

The bottom line is, just because something worked for one person does not mean it will work for you. If you ask three career counselors for advice, you will be lucky to get *only* three different answers! Art; not science. No magic pill.

Your job search is *your* job search. *You* have to decide what is right for *you*. It is all on *you*. That said, you have to be comfortable doing whatever it is that you will be doing otherwise people interacting with you will be suspicious. They will not understand your behavior. The only time you have no choice but to get out of your comfort zone is when networking. More on that later.

No one can get a job for you. You have to get the offer yourself. Yes, people can introduce you. Yes, people can recommend you. Yes, people can help you. But, no, they cannot get the job *for* you. You stand or fall on your own.

If you want to stand, continue reading.

Your Wants

You may think this is a book about how to get a job, and it is, but it is also a marketing book. You have to know how to market yourself to employers. It is also a selling book. You have to know how to sell yourself to employers.

There is an old interview question for someone applying, obviously, for a sales position. The interviewer removes a pen from his pocket, holds it out to the interviewee and orders, "Sell me this pen!"

The normal response is to ask the person why they need a pen. You have to know what your prospect needs in order to know what to say to them, what will resonate with them, how to sell to them. Then the salesperson will speak about benefits and attributes. That's the standard response. You can do that in a job interview. Tell the interviewer about your attributes and the benefits they will derive from hiring you.

1

A more modern response is to tell a story about how the pen helped someone else, in the same demographic as the prospect, so that they can relate to the story. In other words, form an emotional bridge between the prospect and the pen. You can do that in a job interview. Tell a story about a success you had that will resonate with the interviewer and, by so doing, show them not just what type of professional you are, but what type of person you are. (I'll explain how later.) But there's a third option:

I don't remember where I read this, but someone once wrote that the best response, the most effective response, is to take the pen, put it in *your* pocket, and leave the room! Brilliant! Absolutely brilliant! When the interviewer demands the return of their pen, refuse. "You told me to sell you the pen. You gave it to me. As far as I am concerned, if you don't buy it, it is mine to keep. If you want it, give me a dollar." Have a smile on your face, exchange the pen for the dollar and at the end of the meeting, return the dollar. You can do that in a job interview as well. Find a diplomatic way to let the interviewer know that you want to work for them, not their competition. How? Simple. Bring up their competitors once or twice, especially when asked questions about their, the interviewers', company. Convince them that you can solve their problems. Believe me; they'll know that if they don't take you, their competition might. And if they don't realize that truth, why would you want to work for them?

When marketing and selling yourself to a prospective employer you have to show that you are unique. Differentiate yourself from your competition. Dare to walk out with the pen in your pocket! I'll teach you how.

Now let's get started.

Budget. While, as stated, you have to be focused on the employer and not on yourself, that is not so at the beginning of your job search when you have to determine your needs (and, of course, at the end, when the employer has to meet them).

You may want to tell people that you are looking for a job because you want a reason to get up in the morning. Or maybe you say it is because you really enjoy your chosen profession. And that, and all the other legitimate explanations you give may, in fact, really be true. But the bottom line is, you are doing it for the money. And there is nothing wrong with that. The question, of course, is how much do you need?

This is important question because it determines for which jobs you will apply and how you will respond to the question, "What are your salary expectations?" While it deals with the application process, which we cover in Part Two, it is such a common question that I will deal with it now to get it out of the way.

It is really a simple question to answer: If you are currently employed, say, "I am earning X, not including benefits." If you are recently unemployed, say, "I was last earning X, not including benefits." If you have been unemployed for a long time (your definition of "long,"), say, "I need X, not including benefits."

This is not a negotiation; it is simply an answer to a question which will tell the employer if they can afford you. Saying, "not including benefits," means there is room for negotiation (which we will cover in Part Four).

There are people who believe that it is wrong to answer this question which, by the way, as we will discuss, is now illegal in some jurisdictions. They want to play games. "I am flexible." "I am open." I am telling you that those responses do not work. If you don't provide the employer with the information they want, someone else will. Don't play games!

But for now, let's put the focus on you.

You need to know how much you really need to earn. And there is one simple way to find out: Create a budget. That does not answer the question of what you *want*, but rather what you *need*. And, at the end of the process, your needs will become important. (Remember, your budget will show what you need *net*, not *gross*!)

Now we get to your *wants*, those things that are important for you but, nevertheless, are not necessary to pay the bills. These are the things, besides money, that get you up in the morning. They make you feel satisfied. If you need it, they provide you with a refuge from your personal life. Let's digress (As you will see, I do that a lot!) and further explore this.

Work-life Balance. Countless people say that they strive for "work-life balance," meaning that they strive to be fulfilled both professionally and personally. They see it as a zero-sum game. Most see it as a factor of time. Including commute time, they figure they spend 10 hours a day at work. If they sleep for seven hours, that leaves them another seven for family, friends and self. Great in theory, but unrealistic.

Stop thinking about work-life balance. There is no such thing. Sometimes work comes first. Sometimes family comes first.

Sometimes you come first. Yes, you have to miss your daughter's play because you have to meet with the new client from whom, directly or indirectly, you will earn the money to enable your daughter to have what she needs to be in that play. Yes, you can miss the staff meeting because you have to be at your daughter's play because your participation in the meeting will change nothing, but being at the play will help your daughter overcome her stage fright which is crucial for her development.

You *have* to be at the meeting; you *want* to be at the play. Or, you *have* to be at the play; you *want* to be at the meeting. That's the balance. In life you have to balance between "have to"s and "want to"s. You have to finish the report by 6:00 PM. You want to finish reading a book. That's any easy one. The daughter's play is the tough one. But the bottom line is, in the real world, money determines everything and that is an important lesson for your daughter to learn. (Yes, sons too!) You are teaching her priorities. If your job depends on something, the job comes first because it enables you to have the means to take care of your wants – and your children's needs.

Now that we have properly defined "work-life balance," let's consider those professional "wants" that you need to give you that reason to get up in the morning; the things that are more meaningful for you than just earning the money you need to realize your personal needs and wants.

Choosing Where to Work. First, it is important to determine the *type* of place where you want to work. There is no wrong answer. This is a purely personal decision. You have a few options, ignoring self-employment – the "gig economy" – which is beyond the scope of this book:

Start-ups. Technically a case can be made that along with technology and Political Correctness, the "start-up" is a 21st Century creation and the third new thing after technology and Political Correctness. But that is not really so. All businesses begin as start-ups. It's in the name! And whether it is a twenty-first or a twentieth century business, they all face the same things: Concerns over financing and experience.

You have to ask questions: Does the start-up have enough funds on-hand to stay in business for at least two years without any revenue being generated? Do the founders have the experience to, at least theoretically, be successful? To phrase this in the extreme, do they have money and do they know what they are doing? And there is only one way to find out: You have to ask (and then check to see if they are lying!).

Here's the problem: Founders usually see their company through rose-colored glasses. They are going to be the next Google, Amazon, Microsoft, Apple, Uber... You get the idea. But the truth is, they won't. The odds are against them. Most businesses don't last more than a few years. So joining a start-up is a gamble. Can you afford to make that gamble?

Bottom line for-profits. There is nothing wrong with making money. There is nothing wrong with being focused on making money. Plenty of companies are in business to make money for their owners, investors and staff. It is honorable. Why? Because the only way to succeed is to offer quality products or services and to have excellent customer service. If that is the type of company you are interested in, great! But remember one thing: You will be judged on how much revenue and how much profit you contribute to the company's bottom line. It does not matter how much you are liked and respected, if you can't produce, you're gone!

Mission-driven for-profits. There are plenty of companies that have a mission. The mission guides their decision making. A great example are the community-minded B Corps and Benefit Corporations. Yes, you have to produce, but your numbers, so to speak, are tempered by your contribution to making the corporate mission a reality. Allow me to use myself as an example.

In addition to being a career counselor, I am also an executive recruiter. Companies hire me to find staff for them. The mission of my company is to promote the hiring of veterans. Let's say that I had two employees. Employee A closes searches at an unbelievable rate. She is a superstar. Employee B does a great job. He is not as productive as Employee A, but he does great work. Here's the difference. All of Employee A's closes are with candidates who are not veterans. Employee B mainly places veterans. Since I lower my fee by one-third when the candidate is a veteran, Employee B is not contributing to my bottom line at the same level as Employee A.

Let's say I need to promote someone. Who did I promote? I promote Employee B because he understands the company *and* the job. Employee A only understands the job.

Non-profits. For over a decade, on two continents and in three countries, I worked for non-profits. I enjoyed it. The front-line staff, so to speak, did their jobs and the rest took care of profitability. Yes, my friends, non-profits make profits. They have to or they will not stay in business. The difference, for our purposes, between a for-profit and a non-profit is what happens to those profits. In the case of the former, the profits go to the stakeholders; in the case of the latter, they are reinvested in the corporation.

Mainly, I was a fundraiser. So I had to bring in enough money to cover the corporation's expenses, at least in part. But I was also responsible for public relations, working with the media, and community relations. So if one month the money was not pouring in, but we were getting phenomenal press, that was fine. I was doing my job. There definitely was pressure, but there was also balance. And that is what non-profits offer, balance.

Some people coming to me for help with career change tell me that they want to transition from the for-profit to the non-profit sector. Why? Well, as one person told me, "I'm tired of the rat race." My response? "In non-profits you still have a rat race, only the rats are different!"

Instead of crazy, aggravating clients or customers, you now have equally crazy, aggravating donors, board members and volunteers. Members of the public call to complain and blame you for things over which you have no knowledge, no control and no responsibility. You will toss and turn at night. And, until you move up the ladder, you will not be earning as much as your friends in the for-profit world. But if you are the type of person who needs a mission, the type of person who needs to feel that they are part of something with a societal good, I would highly recommend a non-profit career.

Culture. You know how much you need to earn. You know what type of corporation at which you want to work. But will you be successful? That depends on the corporate culture. This is very important and we will touch upon it in more detail when we discuss interviewing. But for now you have to consider atmospherics.

What do I mean?

When you go for an interview you can learn a great deal about the company by using your eyes, ears and nose. Are people (you won't know if they are employees, clients/customers, vendors, investors, board members, guests, etc.) walking around smiling and laughing, or is the atmosphere "cold?" When you look into offices and cubicles, are they sterile or personalized? Is the receptionist prim and proper or friendly and inviting? Is the place clean? Is there an unpleasant odor? What do your senses tell you about the company?

Well, obviously, you can't find out the answers to these questions until you actually get an interview. Or can you? As a matter of fact, while it is not perfect, you can get a pretty good idea about the company from their website, social media, and on-line reviews. But here's the problem:

Websites and social media pages are created by companies to put their best foot forward, and reviews can be suspect. Look carefully. Some things can slip by the censors, so to speak. Perhaps there are videos of company events. Is everyone in business attire or are they casually dressed? That will tell you something.

Clothing matters. Let's take two extremes: IBM and Google. Traditionally, at IBM employees (men, of course) had to wear dark blue suits, white shirts, red ties and black shoes and socks. At Google, they could care less what you wear as long as everything that has to be covered is covered. Where are you on that continuum? Are you closer to IBM or Google?

On-line reviews, on websites like Glassdoor.com, should be read but taken with a grain of salt. A negative review could be from a disgruntled employee. A positive review could be from an employee up for a promotion. And anonymous reviews, as far as I am concerned, are next to worthless. But there is a cumulative effect. If all reviews are negative, and the anonymity appears to be because the reviewer is scared they will lose their job, but they nevertheless want to warn people about the company, it should definitely be a factor in your calculus.

Of course, there are also independent sources. Google the company. Find out what kind of press they have. Are they active in the community? Does their leadership receive awards? Do their products or services receive awards? What is their image? Is this a place where you would be comfortable? That's the question you have to ask yourself.

Type of Job. OK, so you know in your own mind what atmosphere you want. But what type of job. Again, there is no wrong answer.

Do you want a job with specific responsibilities? Do you want to have a variety of responsibilities? Do you want authority? Do you want there to be room for advancement? Do you want on-going training to stay current? You can get answers to these questions by reviewing the LinkedIn Profiles of the company's employees and, of course, confirming what you have learned by asking the interviewers when you get an interview.

Once you have decided the answers to all these questions, you have to start looking for prospective employers.

Research

As a professional in your field you should already know the 20 to 25 companies where you would really like to work. If you are new to the field you will have to do some research. It is not difficult.

Read business publications, especially industry-specific journals or magazines. I highly recommend *Inc.* and *Fast Company.* I read them religiously, every month. While they are general business magazines and not industry-specific, they are treasure troves of information. Go to the public library. They should have directories that you can use for free. It will take time, but it will be time well spent.

If you are a recent college graduate, talk to the people in Career Services. But don't ignore your professors. By definition, they should know what is happening in your industry. After all, they probably were the ones who introduced it to you!

These 20 to 25 companies are your dream employers. You should write to the heads of their Human Resources departments, introducing yourself. Since you have done your research, you know their focus so simply send the following type of email, attaching your résumé:

Subject: Introduction

Ms. Kathy Smith
Vice President, Human Resources
XYZ Corporation
123 Main Street
Anytown, ST 12345

Dear Ms. Smith,

Allow me to take this opportunity to introduce myself in the hope that if a position opens at XYZ for someone with my qualifications, you will consider me.

Having successfully ..., I am confident that I will be able to help XYZ ...

I have taken the liberty of attaching a copy of my résumé for your review.

Thank you in advance for your consideration.

Sincerely,

Jane Doe
123-456-7890

Simple. No meaningless flattery. You tell them what you have done and place it in the context of what they do. That's all that is required. Sadly, don't expect a response. If you get one, great! But your goal is to get into their database. That should satisfy you. If your goal is to immediately get an interview followed by a job offer, you will be disappointed. And whatever you do, don't call them. Assume they got it. HR hates phone calls from résumé submitters!

Be realistic. Working for your dream companies may be just that, a dream. This means you still have to network and respond to ads, two subjects we will address. For now, suffice it to say that the minority of jobs are advertised. Even though they are the minority, you ignore them at your own risk.

Where are the majority of jobs found? Meeting people. It's called "networking," and you have to do it. It's not that *the majority* of jobs are found by networking, it's *the vast majority* of jobs. You have to network, a subject we shall discuss in depth.

Your Internet Presence

Just as you have to do research on possible employers and, as we will discuss in Part Three, on interviewers and the employees of the companies where you will be interviewing, employers, if they are smart, will do their own research – *on you!*

Obviously, the first thing they are going to look at is your résumé. And if you have links to your social media accounts, they should check them out. So don't complain, for example, if they go to your Facebook page and immediately disqualify you. That's on you! You shared the link and you did not make your page private.

Case in point: The father about whom I wrote on LinkedIn who included a link to his daughter's website. Under normal circumstances, a good thing. But his daughter is a pornographer...

In Part Two we will discuss résumés. For now what's important to remember is that your résumé is the gateway to your career – literally! It should include links to whatever you have done on the internet of which you want the recipient of the résumé to be aware. This could or should be your LinkedIn Profile, YouTube videos, Twitter account, Facebook, any other social media platforms, and sites where your work portfolio can be found.

LinkedIn, of course, is professional. Period. End of sentence. End of Discussion. However, you may have used YouTube, Twitter, Facebook and the rest to have fun, express views on hot topics, share photos with friends, etc. In other words, you may have put things on the internet that you really do not want a prospective employer to see. So there is no doubt, foolish behavior on social media sites has cost people job offers, and, while it is not our subject, you should remember this, *their jobs*! Infamously, after President Trump's first address to Congress, one man sent out a tweet criticizing the widow of a member of the US military who had died in battle and who the President had recognized. The entire House stood in her honor and his memory. There was no mention of the man's employer on his Twitter account, but people found him on LinkedIn, contacted his employer, and he was summarily fired.

Bottom line; remove anything you have placed on the internet that may be embarrassing. I am choosing my words carefully because you should not hide who you are. As already stated, "fit" is probably the most important consideration when hiring or accepting a job. You want prospective employers to know who/what you are. But if your photos on Facebook are of you naked, drinking and carousing, and your comments on issues of the day are profanity-laden, if, in other words, your public behavior makes you look like a fool, you are not going to get many job offers and you won't get any, I am convinced, from serious professionals. Clean up your internet presence before you start your job search. It will save you a lot of grief.

Of course, there may be things on the internet about you that you cannot remove because you did not post them. And, there may be things that you placed on the internet that you cannot remove. And they may cost you a job offer. But if given the opportunity to explain the former, simply shrug your shoulders and say, "If only one person on the internet hates me, I can live with that. And I would rather have them attack me than someone who can't take it." This shows maturity.

In the case of the latter, when you placed something stupid on the internet, just shrug your shoulders and say, "I used to be an idiot." The key is, don't try to defend yourself unless you honestly believe that what you wrote was proper. This goes back to "fit." Don't hide who you are, but don't cry if it costs you a job.

While nonsense on the internet may cost your grief, what will give you a lot of joy will be the use you make of LinkedIn – as long as you act professionally. I cannot overemphasize its importance.

LinkedIn

Just so we are clear, if you consider yourself a professional, or if you want others to consider you a professional, you have to have a presence on LinkedIn. You do not need a Premium account. The Basic, free account, will more than suffice. (Everything I mention in this book about LinkedIn relates to the free account.) But you *have* to be on LinkedIn. You can forgo all the other social media sites, but not LinkedIn.

Why? Because professionals are on LinkedIn; it is the best way to be found. Stupid question: What would you prefer, to run after employers or to have employers run after you? So how do we make that happen?

Employers, by definition, cannot run after you if they do not know that you exist. You have to be known. You have to be findable. You cannot be "the best kept secret in town." LinkedIn is where employers and recruiters go to find serious talent.

The starting point is the Profile. The more information in it, the better your chances of being found. You will know if your Profile is effective because, once a week, you will receive a report from LinkedIn telling you who has searched for you and how often you have appeared in search results. In addition to an email, the statistics will also appear on your Homepage and "Dashboard," which are only visible to you.

Now we will review each section of the Profile, starting from the top and work our way down. (Ironically, given the length of this section, I am only giving an overview. The reason is that LinkedIn is always modifying its website. What I write today, I want to be relevant by the time this book is read. Twice I posted "how to" videos on YouTube on using LinkedIn and within a week LinkedIn changed their user interface making the specifics of the videos irrelevant. I don't want that to happen with this book. So I am concerned here more with the *what to do* than the *how to do*. That is also why there are no screenshots.)

When you are in edit mode looking at your Profile, on the right (at least currently it is on the right) you will find "Contact and Personal Information." Fill it out. Definitely include your email, social media accounts and, if you have them, blog and website, but do you really want the world, literally the world, to know your address and phone number? If you are a business, fine, but a private person? Recruiters and employers do not need to call you; an email will more than suffice. (Just make certain to check your SPAM file when you are in job search mode.)

Also, click on "Edit public Profile & URL." First, change the URL for your account. It will default to your name and a series of numbers and letters. Keep it simple. Remove the numbers and letters, and try to make it just your name. If it is not available, add a hyphen and a number or the acronym for your state or anything else that is simple to type. You want to make it easy because your LinkedIn URL will be on your résumé and if someone is reading it on paper, they can't click on the URL! You don't want something as silly as a typo to cost you a job offer.

Additionally, make certain that all sections of your Profile are visible to the public and not just to your first-degree connections. Which brings us to the question of how many first-degree connections you should have. It is your network; its quality and size will determine how effective you will be on LinkedIn and how much influence you will have.

First, an explanation: You and I are directly connected on LinkedIn. We are first-degree connections. You and your cousin are directly connected but your cousin and I are not. Your cousin is a second-degree connection of mine, a first-degree connection of yours. Your cousin and his boss are first-degree connections but she, his boss, is not connected to either of us, making her my third-degree connection and your second-degree connection. Got it?

The maximum number of first-degree connections a member can have is 30,000. I have 30,000. At this moment my entire network of first-, second- and third-degree connections is exactly 7,170,293 individuals. In other words, when I do something on

LinkedIn, I have a *potential* reach of millions. Think about what that means.

In any event, there are many people who only want to have a selected network on LinkedIn. They are concerned, for example, that people will be able to see their first-degree connections and reach out to them. That's easy to deal with. Under "Settings" it is possible to limit who can see your connections. But these are legitimate concerns and there is no right or wrong answer. You may be selective or, like me, you may welcome the world. Just keep in mind, when you reject someone as a first-degree connection, you are also rejecting all of their first-, second-, and third-degree connections, current *and future*.

In addition to my 30,000 first-degree connections, I also have 2,269 additional followers (all first-degree connections are automatically followers, although they can choose to "unfollow" a first-degree connection and still remain first-degree connections). So when I post something on LinkedIn, an update, a photo or an article, terms I will explain in a moment, it reaches, potentially, over 32,000 people directly, and by extension, possibly millions. I receive reports from LinkedIn about the number of views or reads my posts get. The ironic thing is that in some cases, more of my updates, photos or articles are seen by second- or third-degree connections than by my first-degree connections. How is that possible?

When, for example, you publish an article, after you click "Publish," you will be instructed to index your article by assigning hash tags. If I were to do it for this book I might write, #jobsearch #networking #résumés #coverletters #interviewing. Additionally, you will be given the opportunity to send out a Tweet announcing the publication of your article. Do it. Include in the tweet, "Tip @LinkedInEditors." This will inform the people in charge of LinkedIn Pulse (the name for the blogs on the site), that the article has been published and they may decide to include it in industry news feeds which will promote your article to untold millions.

Whenever anyone "likes" something you do on LinkedIn, their first-degree connections may be (nothing is definite and no one knows who or when a notification of a "like" will reach someone) informed of the "like" and then they may look at what was "liked" and then, if they "like" it, *their* first-degree connections will be notified, and then the process continues *ad infinitum*. I have had updates read by thousands of people, and some by only a few. I have had articles read by only a dozen or so individuals and others read by tens of thousands and, once, by over a hundred thousand. That's how you become known. With a small network, it is unlikely to happen.

It is important, so I will repeat myself: When you reject someone's invitation to join their network, you are rejecting all of their first-, second- and third degree connections, current *and future*. Since you can always request a first-degree connection to introduce you to one of their first-degree connections, by extension, you may also be rejecting the very person who could help you today or tomorrow.

One other thing to consider: If you have a first-degree connection who works at a company where you will be interviewing, or if they have a first-degree connection working there or, for that matter, who worked there in the past, you can reach out to them for advice. If you are not connected, you can't! When reaching out, never ask for a reference, they don't know you and it's unprofessional. But I have found that if you introduce yourself and ask general, open-ended questions about corporate culture, a meaningful conversation can ensue. Just don't abuse the relationship.

Now let's get to the Profile, again, starting from the top. (I am using mine as the model. Some people rearrange their sections, when the system permits it.)

Background photo. You don't have to have one, but you should. And if at all possible it should send a message. Using Paint or a similar program, you could have as your background photo some inspirational quote. (Be careful of copyrights.) Or it could be a shot of you in action. Perhaps speaking on a stage or in front of an audience. In my case, it is a shot of my appearance on the Fox Business Channel. Regardless of what you choose, you want it to complement the message you are sending in your Profile, namely that you are a professional worthy of respect and consideration.

Headshot. Overlaid on the background photo will be your headshot. And that is what it should be, a clear photo of you and only you. Not your family. Not you and your best friend. Not your dog or cat. You. And you today, not 20 years ago.

We will discuss discrimination later, but for now, I had a career counseling client who was very concerned about his age. After we edited his Profile, I told him to upload his photo. When he had finished, he sent me the link. I'm no good with names, and I am almost as bad with faces. I had not seen him in a couple of weeks, but even I knew something was not right.

I called him and asked about the photo. He told me it was the best he had and that it have been taken 20 years earlier! When I asked him why he would use such an old photo, he told me he was worried about age discrimination. Then I asked him how he thought interviewers would react when he showed up and they saw the current him. Use a recent photo.

Of course there are photos and then there are photos. One woman did an experiment. She posted a very attractive picture of herself; a professional headshot. She called it her "pretty pic." Then she posted another photo, replacing the first. This one she called "ugly pic." It was a shot of her speaking while wearing a microphone like the ones anchors wear on television when hosting events. So there was a "ball," if you will, in front of her mouth and an "arm" across her cheek on the end of which was the "ball." During a one-month period, her Profile with the "pretty" photo was viewed 900 times. When she changed to the "ugly" photo, her Profile was viewed only 500 times, but she got more business from the "ugly" than from the "pretty" photo. Keep that in mind when choosing your photo. You are not on LinkedIn to get a date; you are on LinkedIn to get a job or for career advancement.

(Just as an aside, and we will get to messaging later, you can always message someone in your industry if you are working on a project and have a question. I know one person who was working on his first "landmark building." He reached out to an architect in his network and asked a question. Then he posted the question in one of his LinkedIn Groups (we'll discuss those as well). Within 24 hours he had his answer and had made a number of new colleagues.)

Name. Many people think that adding symbols, like stars or check marks, makes their Profile more noticeable. It might, but not in a good way. I don't think it is very professional. More importantly, sometimes LinkedIn gets a little antsy and symbols can mess up a search when someone is looking for a person by name. If they are just doing a generic search, it shouldn't matter.

In any event, you may want to use your middle initial to differentiate yourself from others with your same first and last name. Some people like to include professional titles – MD, Ph.D. MBA – after their names. That may mess up a search if the system recognizes "MD" as the person's last name, but it is impressive. But be sensible about it. First, limit yourself to one or two designations. Too many and you come across as a bit pompous. And don't use the designation if it is not directly related to your goals. If you no longer wish to practice medicine, don't broadcast the fact that you are an MD. By all means, include it under "Education," but you don't want employers asking themselves, "What's a physician doing looking for work as a project manager?"

For the record, I don't use "Ph.D." on my Profile name. My degree is in International Relations. I am proud of it. I have had many academic accomplishments and I learned a great deal, perhaps most importantly how to right good and prufreed even better. (Friends, don't lose your sense of humor. Being able to laugh at yourself is an important component of a successful job search, just as it is in life in general. I have found that job seekers who take everything too seriously have a difficult time finding employment because they don't know how to relax.) Additionally, I was taught researching, public speaking, decision making, organization and analysis, all skills crucial to being a successful professional in any field. But that was a past life, so while I use it on the cover of this book, and it is listed in my Profile under "Education," I don't use it after my name.

Women who change their names after marrying sometimes include their maiden name. It's a good idea. Someone may remember her under her former name, not knowing her current one.

Headline. Immediately under your name appears the "Headline." In a Profile, everything is important, to varying degrees, but the Headline may be the most important component. Some people say to include your profession. Some people say not to. I say, you have 120 characters, including spaces, to sell yourself, so prioritize. This may be the only thing, other than your name, current place of employment and location, that anyone actually reads!

First, in my case I make it clear that I am a recruiter and career counselor. But I also am a speech writer. But I am not just any speech writer; I can honestly say that I am a five-star rated speech writer on Fiverr. So after "recruiter and career counselor," I inserted a "•" and added "'5-Star' speech writer on Fiverr.'" (I use the "•" to separate the different sections of the Headline to make it easier to read.) I have 30,000 first degree connections which means I cannot accept new connections. It also means I am very well connected.

That is what I want people to know, especially potential career counseling clients because I may be able to introduce them to someone. Accordingly, I have included "30K" in my Headline. Next comes mention of my being a podcast host. This might be of interest to entrepreneurs who have a story they want to share, literally, with the world. And finally, the mission of my company is to promote the hiring of veterans so I end with, "We hire veterans!"

What really is the Headline? A quick introduction and then your unique selling proposition(s). Recruiter, career counselor. Five-star speech writer. Well connected. Has a podcast. Supports veterans. That's me in a nutshell.

But there is another way to write the headline. Sometimes a clear statement of what you have to offer will do the trick. (Remember, I am looking for business; you are looking for employment!)

Let's say you are a controller. You could write, "Controller with 15 years of experience reducing expenses in Manufacturing sector." That will fit with room to spare. But I think this sounds better: "Controller • Last year I saved my employer $10 million. Do you need savings?" Or, "Controller who last year saved his employer $10 million. How much did your controller save you?"

So to summarize, you want your Headline to be a quick introduction followed by your unique selling proposition. And if you can combine the two, so much the better.

As a job seeker you should also consider including in the Headline, "Open to New Opportunities." That way everyone seeing your Profile will know you are on the market. But beware; this is a zero-sum game. The more people who know you are looking, the less confidentiality you have. And if your current employer finds out...

The next sections are straightforward. Under **Current Position** you, obviously, choose your current position. When you create your Profile, LinkedIn will prompt you to complete the various sections. It is not a big deal. As you are following the prompts, you will enter your various jobs, current and past. It's very simple. The system automatically inserts, under your Heading, your current place of employment, where you last went to school, your location, and the number of first-degree connections you have, up to 500.

Education. List the schools you attended, the years, and your major. It is important to include all of the schools because, as noted, someone may want to search for alumni of your school. If it is not there, you will not appear in the search results.

I know of one person who was found because the person looking for them remembered the name of the school (they had been classmates), the years they were there, but not the person's name. They found them and offered them a job.

From the drop-down menu, choose the most relevant school from which you graduated. That could be the school where you received your highest degree or the most recent, if you went back to school to supplement your education, degree or certification.

Country, ***Zip Code*** and ***Location*** are all straightforward, but not so for ***Industry***. You have to choose from the list LinkedIn provides. (Ironically, "Industry" is no longer visible on Profiles. It is, however, one of the required items when setting up an account and critical to appearing in relevant search results.) You might not find your specific industry. For example, there is no "Sales" option; you have to use "Marketing and Advertising." But the important thing to remember is to use *your* industry, not your employer's. For example, if you are an accountant working at an IT company, your industry is not "Information Technology and Services," but rather "Accounting." Why? Because the entire purpose of LinkedIn is to be found. If an employer is looking for an accountant, they are not going to do a search for "Information Technology and Services;" they are going to search for professionals who have listed their profession as "Accounting" and are located in the relevant city or region, as the case may be. (In metropolises, you can list, for example, "Greater New York City," without having to be more specific.)

Which brings me to the question of how LinkedIn is used by recruiters and employers. (I do not understand why, but on LinkedIn, this was very controversial.)

There are recruiters and employers who spend their time mining LinkedIn. I do not. Frankly, when I am working on a search, I need to find quality candidates quickly. If I am spending my time reading LinkedIn Profiles, my clients, seeing that I never ask for an exclusive arrangement, may find someone on their own. I have to work fast. I have to work smart. So what do I do?

I do a search of my 30,000 first-degree connections with two search parameters, "Location" and "Industry." That is all I care about.

Let's say I am conducting a search for a client in Manhattan. They are looking for a director of Marketing. I will search within "Greater New York City" for everyone in "Marketing and Advertising." Why don't I narrow the search further? Simple. I do not want to miss out on someone who might be able to help me.

When the search results appear, I send a message to each of my first-degree connections who appear in the results, that goes something like this:

> *Jane,*
>
> *I hope you are well.*
>
> *I wanted to let you know about a search I am working on for a company in Manhattan that is looking to hire a director of Marketing. The job description appears below. If you happen to know of anyone who might be interested, I would appreciate your sharing this message with them.*
>
> *Thanks in advance. I appreciate your efforts,*
>
> *Bruce*

I cut and paste it to everyone, just changing the name. It does not take that long, but even if there are hundreds of messages to send, it is time well spent.

(A slight digression: You can send a message to up to 50 people at a time. Don't do it! It is annoying because whenever anyone responds, the response goes to all 50! It's like hitting "Reply to All." The only thing recipients can do is opt out of the "conversation." Send individual messages. It's better.)

And that's it. I don't ask them if they are interested. I made that mistake in the past. If the job is junior to their current position, they sometimes get nasty. So I ask if they *know of anyone* for the job. If they are personally interested, they will send me their résumé. If not, and they know of someone, they'll forward the message. If not, and they don't know of anyone, nothing will happen.

If they are interested, I need to see their résumé. If their friend is interested, I need to see *their* résumé. There is never any need for me to look at a Profile until I have screened the candidate. Why?

Now we are getting into a bit of a legal issue and I remind you that I am not an attorney.

If I look at a candidate's Profile, I will see their photo. Based on that photo I may be able to identify some of their protected statuses: Gender, race, and possibly their religion. I do not want anyone to ever think that that information goes into my decision about whether or not to interview someone. So I do not look at Profiles until I have screened the candidate over the phone. Then, when we have scheduled an in-person or a Skype interview, I can ask them about any inconsistencies between their Profile and their résumé, and also about anything unique that they have included on their Profile, such as audio files or PDFs. But until I have scheduled an appointment to see them, I don't want to see them!

This does not mean you do not want your Profile to be complete. It should be. You should consider it your personal website. You want employers to engage with it and with you, just at the right time.

But before we get to that, let's pause to consider how to find a job using LinkedIn. It's rather simple: First, join LinkedIn Groups in your profession and see what jobs are posted. Second, click on "Jobs" from your home page and do a search for what you are looking for and where. Third, when the "Jobs" page opens, find "Career Interests" and complete the form activating the "Let recruiters know you are open" switch. And again, on your Headline, include "Open to New Opportunities," if confidentiality is *not* a concern.

About Groups, you can join up to 50. Don't just join Groups relevant to your industry or profession. If you have an interest or hobby, join a few related Groups. First, you will hopefully enjoy the conversations, and, secondly, you may meet someone who can help you.

In Groups, you will not only find job listings but also "Discussions." Join in. Start some. Technically, a "Discussion" can simply be you posting a link to one of your LinkedIn articles or an article in which you were quoted. (More on that in a moment.) It is a great way to get increased "reads" and to meet people. As you will see, interacting with people on LinkedIn can lead to real-world connections and opportunities.

Now let's return to the Profile.

The next section is your ***Summary***. Use strong positive words to describe what you have done, but do not engage in self-praise.

You would never, at least I hope you would never, introduce yourself as a, "highly regarded, consummate professional..." It would sound ridiculous. It also *reads* ridiculous.

What you want to do is to talk about results. List your key accomplishments. And if you follow my résumé model, it will be easy to do. You can cut and paste from your résumé into your Profile. Why reinvent the wheel?

Some people will say that your LinkedIn Profile should not be a repeat of your résumé. I disagree. The one thing you do not want is for there to be any significant differences or inconsistencies between the two. The résumé is a legally binding document; the LinkedIn Profile is not. So the *foundation* of the Profile should be your résumé.

In the Summary, as well as the employment-related listings, you can add links to videos, audio files, PDFs and, in the future, no doubt, more. Do it! It's a great way to let employers know your style. It makes you a "complete" candidate, so to speak.

After the Summary section, LinkedIn automatically inserts and populates another section, ***Your Articles & Activities***. As mentioned, you can post "Updates." Think of them as long tweets of 1,300 characters and spaces. You can also upload photos, including verbiage. And, most importantly, you can write and publish articles, also known as "posts." In the articles you can include photos and links to multi-media. While at all times respecting confidentiality, and avoiding non-professional related controversy, write about your work, profession and industry. Readers will comment. Engage with them; don't debate with them. That's how you will get a following.

It is debatable which is more effective in building a personal brand, updates or articles. They both are. Some things are better suited for the former than the later. It's a question of length. Updates are limited; articles are not. Moreover, updates only remain connected to your Profile for a month; articles remain indefinitely.

You can use updates to promote articles in which you were quoted (We will get to that in a moment), as well as your own articles. In the case of the former, be modest. Don't draw attention to the fact that you were quoted. Just praise the reporter by name (so they will see it and, hopefully, will use you again!) and say something positive about the article. If someone realizes you were quoted, great! If not, what does it matter? You want to be known as a source for good information. That is why you should send links to articles you find online. By all means, comment, don't just forward the link. Let people in your profession know you are a thinker. Instead of giving an opinion, it may actually be better to refrain from doing so directly. Pose questions. It may be better to come across as intellectual rather than opinionated.

Of course, you can comment on other people's updates (Literally, as I am writing this, I just noticed that LinkedIn changed "updates" to "ideas" and added "videos" to the things you can share! See what I mean about keeping this to an overview?), photos and articles posted by other people. The more active you are, the more people will know you.

A note of caution: First, don't be rude. By all means disagree with someone. I disagreed with one person who, after writing back and forth for a few months, ended up inviting me to appear with him on a panel. In other words, my "virtual" network became a real-world network. Remember this when we discuss networking.

Second, people will disagree with you and some will be rude and insulting. It is very hard, and I am guilty of not following my own advice, but, do as I say, not as I do: Don't engage them. You won't win. The only thing you should do is to politely thank them for voicing their opinion and, if appropriate, ask them for the source of whatever it is they are claiming. That usually shuts them up! And when you post on LinkedIn (or, for that matter, any social media site), make certain that you always include your source(s), that way you will have credibility.

Also, keep in mind that when anyone – rude or polite – comments on your posts, just as with "likes," their first-degree connections will be informed. In the case of the rude, it could very well be that their connections will agree with you and not with them. (Of course, the opposite is also true!) In any event, they are all helping you build your brand, which is precisely why you should be on LinkedIn.

To return to our previous discussion about résumés, the important difference between the résumé and the LinkedIn Profile is that the one thing you can do on a Profile that you cannot do on a résumé is to add media and, for that matter, links to articles in which you have been quoted, and online accounts, such as GitHub, where you store a portfolio of your work. For example, if you go to my Profile you will find links to podcasts and YouTube videos, including my television appearances.

Ironically, I have not included links to my press coverage. The reason is that I have been quoted in hundreds of articles; including all of them might be considered overkill! Granted, I could include the most recent, but I have so much already I don't want to overdo it. But consider including some, especially when you are just getting started.

Let's talk about my press coverage:

Since 2010, I have been quoted in 727 articles, appearing in 496 publications, across the United States and in 27 foreign countries, of which I know. To be totally honest, I ain't that good! So how did I do it?

Help A Reporter Out. It's a great website. The URL is www.helpareporter.com. HARO, as it is called, brings together reporters and experts. Sign up as a "source" and, under Settings, choose the categories that interest you. (For the record, it's free!)

The beauty of this site is that you are not pitching to reporters, producers or editors. They are inundated with pitches and, 99 times out of a hundred, those pitches wind up in the "circular file" under their desks, or are deleted from their Inboxes, as the case may be. You might think that your story is newsworthy, but, truth be told, it isn't. Unless you have a contact at the newspaper, magazine, radio or television station, you are wasting your time trying to make it onto the evening news, literally or figuratively.

With HARO, the process is reversed. The reporters, in essence, pitch *you* and therefore you know you have a decent chance of getting press coverage. It is worth the effort. I know because that is how I started my career counseling practice. Readers of my quotes called asking for help. The rest, as they say, is history.

Three times a day, every weekday, you will receive lists of questions from reporters, as well as requests for guests to be on podcasts, radio and television shows. The questions cover every conceivable, and a few inconceivable, topics. When you know the answer, respond quickly because once a reporter has enough answers, they write their article and move on. Also, keep your answers concise so the reporter will not have to edit. In other words, make things simple for them. At the end of your response, tell the reporter that if they send you a link to the article, you will share it with your network. Of course, I can say that I have a total network, combining LinkedIn, Twitter and Facebook, of 38,000 followers. If you have been selective in building your networks, and only have a few hundred or thousand or so followers, and the reporter has to choose between the two of us, who do you think she will choose?

A couple of extra points: First, read the query carefully and make certain you are qualified to respond. Next, establish your credentials so the report knows why she should consider your opinion. Finally, pay no attention to the publication. I have been quoted in, among others, *USA Today*, *US News & World Report*, and *The Wall Street Journal*. I have also been quoted on websites and blogs of which no one has ever heard. But the truth is, I have gotten more business from the latter than the former.

Reporters do not always let you know when they have published, so you may not know about their article unless you find it yourself. Set up a Google Alert for your name (alerts.google.com) placing your name in quotation marks so you won't be notified when anyone with your first or last name is mentioned on the internet. The system is not perfect so, on a weekly basis, Google yourself. (Remember to place your name in quotation marks.) Even if you don't use HARO, this is still a good policy because, as already mentioned, employers may Google you and you need to be aware of what they may find.

Once you have the URL for the article, share it as an "Update." If it is less than 280 characters, and you have connected your Twitter account to your LinkedIn account, it will also be a tweet! Potentially, anyone in your network can see it. Everyone looking at your Profile will see it.

The next sections of the Profile are *Experience*, *Education*, and *Volunteer Experience*.

Under **Experience**, you will be asked for your title, the name of your employer, and when you worked there. Then you have the opportunity to describe your role and accomplishments. Again, cut and paste from the résumé. Also, add relevant multi-media or files. It is always advisable to not just describe something, but to show it.

Education means formal education from accredited institutions. List the name, the major, and the years you attended. That will suffice. We will discuss the issue of including years when we get to the résumé.

Volunteer Experience, as we will discuss later, may actually get you a job. Include your title, the name of the organization, membership dates, and, if you had a function, describe it, focusing on results.

You can add additional sections by clicking on "Add new Profile sections" on the right side of the edit mode screen. No doubt, knowing LinkedIn, by the time you read this, the sections will change. So add what you think is important for you to get the message across that you are that "complete" professional which any employer would want on their team.

For now the sections include, *Publications, Certifications, Patents, Courses, Projects, Honors & Awards, Test Scores, Languages*, and *Organizations*. Let's consider each in turn.

Publications. If you have any publications, by all means, list them. They are proof that editors of professional, academic or media publications think your opinions are important. This is proof to employers that you are truly a recognized expert, if not a leader, in your field.

Certifications. If you have them, list them. Since there is no specific section for licenses, include them as well. They could be the one thing that an employer or recruiter searches for when looking for candidates.

Patents. Patents prove that you are entrepreneurial, innovative and someone who an employer *needs* and not just *wants* since they really may need the rights to whatever it is for which you received the patent. Why wouldn't you include it?

Courses. As opposed to "Education," I see this section as designed for unaccredited studies, or studies not resulting in a degree, certification or license. If you have taken courses, list them. Let employers know that you are current in your field. This is especially true for "older" candidates and the long-term unemployed, because it shows they are active, not idle.

Projects. This is very important. You can get into the details of projects on which you have worked. This could be crucial for project management, IT development, and similar positions.

Honors & Awards. A LinkedIn Profile is no time for modesty. List your honors and awards. They are proof that other people, besides your mother, think that you are exceptional.

Test Scores. Frankly, I think this is a bit much. On the other hand, if you scored 100 in Calculus...

Languages. In today's day and age of a global economy, speaking foreign languages is very important. If you are looking for work in the US, and you don't speak English, forget it. If you are in the States, and speak foreign languages, that means you may be able to open up foreign markets to employers. There is no good reason not to include the languages you speak on your Profile.

Organizations. Given that there is a section on "Volunteer Experience," this section is a bit redundant. If you just pay dues, and are not active, this would be the place to list your memberships

An additional section is **Featured Skills & Endorsements**. You can list up to 50 skills that you possess and then your connections can "endorse" you for some or all. Of course, if you only have a small network, you will not have that many endorsements. No worries. I have thousands and they mean nothing. Why? People use to endorse me and then send me a message, "I just endorsed you for 'Career Counseling.' Please endorse me for X." Or my favorite, "If you endorse me for X, I'll endorse you for whatever you want." I never agreed. As a recruiter I am telling you that "endorsements" on LinkedIn mean nothing. They won't be held against you and they won't be used in your favor. However, the next section may.

Recommendations. For someone to recommend you they have to send you the recommendation and then you decide whether or not to accept it. (Endorsements are automatically included on your Profile and you may not even know about them.) Many a time strangers have offered to recommend me if I would recommend them. I never agreed. That is why I do not give "Recommendations" much value, but I do give them some. There is a condition; the person has to be able to place me in touch with the "recommender" so that I can confirm that the recommendation is legit.

I once had a candidate for an executive recruiting client harp on the number of recommendations he had on his Profile. He had over one hundred! Way too many! I did not believe him for a minute. I printed out the first ten recommendations and asked him for the contact information of the "recommenders." He told me he did not have the information with him. No problem. I told him to email me the information when he got home and I would choose three to contact. I also promised to let him know which ones I would be contacting so that he could speak with them in advance. Needless to say, I never heard from him again.

When a recruiter or an employer wants a recommendation, they want to *hear* the recommendation, not read it on LinkedIn.

Accomplishments. Unlike the "Summary" at the top, this is the place to brag. Brag! Don't be shy. It's alright. And get into the weeds. Let prospective employers know the details of your accomplishments. As already mentioned, you can do the same if you decide to include a *Project* section. The details that you can include, in addition to the multimedia links, are what will differentiate your LinkedIn Profile from your résumé.

The last section, which LinkedIn will insert, **Interests**, lists the individuals and companies you follow, and the Groups to which you belong. As already noted, the advantage of joining Groups is that it is a great way to promote your activities on LinkedIn, especially your articles and those of others in which you have been quoted, but you may also be able to "message" Group members with whom you are not first-degree connections. This can be very valuable and brings me to our last topic, messaging.

Messaging. While not on your Profile, this is important because it is a way for you to interact with your connections confidentially. But be careful. LinkedIn is neither Twitter not Facebook. No one is going to take you seriously if you do not spell correctly, use proper grammar, and write coherently. If you want to be treated like a professional, write like one.

All other forms of communication are visible to all of your connections and, if you so choose, potentially to the over 400 million members of LinkedIn and, via Twitter, even more.

Since we are here, and even though we touched on this briefly when discussing building a network, I sometimes am asked if it is appropriate to contact connections who work at the companies to which you have applied. It can be, but wait until you have an actual interview. Never ask for a recommendation or for permission to use their names. Remember, they are strangers, not real connections. That said, you can tell them that you will be interviewing and ask them general questions. Most people are not offended. In fact, most are glad to offer advice.

When you are successful interacting with members on LinkedIn, as I told you happened to me, that is when your "virtual" network becomes your "real-world" network. That has to be your ultimate goal when joining LinkedIn. Which brings us to perhaps our most important topic, next to interviewing, networking.

Networking

To repeat myself, because it is worth repeating, you have to network because the majority of jobs are not advertised and the only way you will hear about them is if someone tells you about them. It is as simple as that.

What is "networking?" It is important that we define the term. It is *not* exchanging business cards. *Networking is building relationships.* Period. End of sentence. End of discussion.

I need to slightly digress. Do not underestimate the importance of dumb luck. That's how some people get jobs. For example, one of my Millennial clients, a woman who relaxes by doing martial arts, could not get a job. It wasn't her fault; it was the economy. She had a degree in Marketing and spoke Italian. One evening, she went to her dojo and had a match with another woman. She broke her arm. My client accompanied her to the hospital and stayed until her parents arrived. The injured woman's father took my client home. In the car they chatted. Turned out, he was looking for someone to help his company with marketing. Additionally, he had just gotten his first European client, an Italian company. When he heard what degree she had, and that she spoke Italian, he hired her there and then on the spot! (For the record, don't go out and start breaking peoples' arms!)

Everything you do with people, every interaction you have with anyone, is a networking event. I was walking in Manhattan pass *Junior's*, the purveyors of the best cheese cake known to man. There was a young couple walking near me. I heard the woman say, "I hate their cheese cake." I turned around, looked at her boy friend, and said, "Dump her!" After a short discussion, they both became career counseling clients. (This is also why you must always have business cards on you. More on that later.)

My point is this: If you spend all of your time sitting in front of your computer, if you never get out of your house, you will never get lucky! (Come on! You know what I mean! Shame on you!)

In order to build a relationship with someone – given that for present purposes your goal is to find employment – you need three things. And they take time to establish. Networking is a process. It never happens over night. What are those three things? First, the person has to like you. Second, they have to trust you. Third, they have to respect you.

No one worth knowing is ever going to recommend a stranger for a job. It simply will not happen. There has to be a relationship. For a relationship to form they have to like you. Then they have to trust you because they will not want to be embarrassed by you. And finally, for them to actually be proactive and introduce you to their boss, a friend or even an acquaintance, they must respect you. So it is incumbent upon you to get to know them, or rather, for them to get to know you.

The only way for that to happen is by following-up with them and following-through on their advice. But before we get into the weeds, so to speak, I know what many of you are saying to yourselves: "I can't introduce myself to strangers. It's too hard."

You are not alone. The majority of people, when asked what their Number One fear was, said, "Public Speaking." And networking is a form of public speaking. Believe me, I know your fear. I had it. I still have it but I have learned to manage it. I manage the fear; the fear does not manage me.

Ironically, I can speak to a room full of people without the slightest nervousness, but to go over and introduce myself to a stranger at an event – I'd rather undergo root canal without Novocain!

The first time I went to a networking event after I started my business, I had to force myself to introduce myself to other attendees. I set a goal of collecting five business cards. It took me three hours! Next time the goal was 10 cards and it only took me two hours! After that I was, more or less, alright. I realized that whatever fears I had were in my head, not in the room where the event was taking place.

That by the way is true not only when networking but also when interviewing. You can be your own worst enemy. Clear you head of foolishness. No, the woman you approach at a networking event is not going to slap your face because she thinks you are hitting on her. (That one was for my male readers.) No, the man interviewing you is not going to ask why... Sorry, ladies, I can't think of anything. But I know you can! Why, because we all have nonsense in our heads. Get rid of it!

Like anything else, networking takes practice. The more you do it the more comfortable you will be. I have some simple rules for overcoming shyness. They worked for me; I hope they will work for you.

1. Arrive early. Introduce yourself to the host. They will be busy so they will "hand you off" to another early arriver. That will help to ease your tension.

2. Arrive early. If you can't find the host, just walk over to someone who also arrived early. It will be less daunting to go over to one of a handful of people than to walk over to a stranger in a room full of people.

3. Look for your own kind. No, I don't mean members of your racial, religious, age or other group. Look for the scared! You know who they are. They are the ones who are looking out the window pretending to be interested in the view. Or they are standing in the center of the room playing with their phones. Now if they are in a corner, they may not be "playing" but working, so those people you should leave alone. Finally, if they are standing anywhere, looking at the crowd, smiling, they are probably praying that someone will come over and put them out of their misery. Do it!

4. Set a goal for yourself. Mine was collecting a certain number of business cards. Try it.

5. Lastly, and we will discuss this in more detail shortly, follow-up.

A question I get all the time is, "How do you get into a conversation that is taking place with a group of people?" In other words, you look around and people are standing in groups. How do you join in? Simply walk over, stand a couple of feet away and glance at the people you are facing. If none of them acknowledges you, move on. Try another group. Listen to their conversation. If you have something to add, remain and wait for your chance. If you have nothing to contribute, move on. Just don't interrupt. That would be rude. Standing and listening is not. In fact, by not acknowledging you, they are the ones who are being rude. Do you really want to network with rude people?

Before we go any further, we have to look at the issue of communication and body language, relevant for both networking and interviewing:

You might think that the words you speak are the major component of your communication with other people when you meet in the real world (typing being the major component online). Well, you would be wrong.

Preparing

Research clearly shows that our body language is the most significant part of our verbal communication (55%), followed by our tone of voice (38%), and coming in last, our actual words (7%). That's right, what we say is less important than how we appear when saying it, and how we say it.

Think about it. When someone is looking at the floor while speaking to you, are you convinced of their sincerity or do you have doubts? When someone is looking you straight in the eyes but their tone of voice is blasé, do you believe them? Of course you don't. That is why, and we will return to this when we discuss interviewing, you have to be certain that your body language and tone of voice complement your words. But there is more to it than that.

We all send subliminal messages. We are not consciously aware of them, and we can't manipulate them, but we all have minute facial tics that our brains pick up on when we look at someone. That is why we sometimes feel an instant like or dislike for a person we have not met or to whom we have not spoken. By being charming you sometimes can overcome that initial reaction. That said, you can visibly turn someone off by the way you stand and the way you look.

While not always true, you can send a message that you are not interested in meeting someone if you are standing with your legs together, arms crossed, and have a frown on your face. Do it and no one is going to come near you!

So do the opposite: Stand with your legs comfortably apart, one arm at your side and the other slightly bent, and grin. That sends the not so subliminal message that you are a warm and inviting person. Try it. It really works!

Hopefully, I don't have to say this but, dress professionally. You will be treated the way you look. Remember, you are trying to impress people. If, and I have seen this, you are a man and your shirt tail is sticking out of your trousers, your tie is loose, and your collar is crooked, no one is going to want to form a relationship with you. Same thing, and I have also seen this, with a woman whose clothes are too revealing. If you look like a bum you will be treated like a bum. If you look like a... Well, you get the idea.

And please, never wear perfume or cologne. Don't try to smell good; try not to smell at all! The French invented perfume because they did not want to bathe. Take a bath! Just because you think the perfume or cologne has a pleasant scent does not mean others will.

And if a person literally can't stomach being near you, they are not going to want to network with you, not to mention interview you. Don't do it!

Moving on, you have to find worthwhile networking events. Those are events where there are employed professionals and business owners in your field or in the field in which you are interested.

Now that is not necessarily true. There are exceptions to every rule. If you need to practice networking, go to Meetup.com and find an event in your area that sounds interesting. Attend and practice. If you make a fool out of yourself, who cares? If you are like me, the first time you go over to someone, you probably will make a fool of yourself! But by the end of the event, you will learn from your mistakes and you will be just fine.

Theoretically, you could actually meet someone at a non-professional event who could help you. But don't do what many of my career counseling clients did before meeting me. When I would tell them that they have to network, they would protest that they had been networking but to no avail. Then, in response to my question, they told me that they had gone to networking events for job seekers. While theoretically a job seeker may know of a job opening that may be of interest to you, in most cases you are, by definition, competitors. Why would a job seeker in your profession help you get a job? OK, theoretically, you may be in same profession but not looking for the same job. Or you may be at different levels, they may be senior, you may be junior. But seriously, do you think anything will come of it. Maybe long-term, but if you need a job now? I don't think so.

So how do you find events where you can find worthwhile networking opportunities? Ironically, start with Meetup, look at your "Community Calendar," and simply Google "X networking events in Y," where X is your profession or industry and Y is your place of residence. (Who would ever have thought that I would be using Algebra? I guess I have to apologize to my math teacher. I did not believe him when he said that one day it would be useful!) You will be surprised by what you find. I know it works because I have done it.

Do not ignore career fairs and business expos. Especially for college students and persons looking for entry-level positions, career fairs are great. And the good news is that most people don't have a clue what they are doing. I used to attend many and I gave up. Practically no one ever followed up with me. So all you have to do to differentiate yourself is to send a thank-you email to the people you meet attaching a copy of your résumé. That is in case they did not ask you to do something specific, like complete an application form online. And if they did, after you complete the task, whatever it is, thank them and inform them that you followed-through.

Remember, the people you meet at career fairs almost always work in Human Resources. Those are the people you need. So what if they don't have something for you then and there on the spot? Tomorrow they may and, if you have followed-up with them, acted professionally, they may very well remember you.

The opposite is the case with business expos. The people there are almost always in Sales or Marketing. They probably don't know of any openings, but you never know. In any case, business expos are a good place to practice networking, meaning introducing yourself and talking about yourself to strangers. If you mess up, it won't matter. But you won't and you will have the business card of someone who may be able to open doors for you. So follow-up with them the way I am about to explain.

But before I get to that, make certain that you do not forget your existing network. Your friends, families, former colleagues, schoolmates and service providers, not to mention the members of any religious, civic or professional organizations with which you are involved. Contact everyone you know. I promise you that the one person who you choose not to inform of your job search will be the one person who could have actually connected you to your next job.

My favorite networking story: A father, a controller, lost his job. His 10-year old daughter's best friend's father was a CFO. She asked her father for his résumé. He gave it to her and she, as she had promised him, gave the résumé to her friend and she gave it to her father. You can guess what happened. Tell *everyone* you are looking for work because you will never know who might have been able to help you.

A word of explanation: By "service providers" I mean the professionals you interact with on a regular basis. Ever spend a few minutes at the dry cleaners? Do it some time. Customers, especially at the end of the day, talk. The owner is like a bartender. They know what is going on. So does your mechanic. So does your barber. So does your hairdresser.

The one person who is usually ignored, and who should never be ignored, is your rabbi, priest, minister or imam. Spiritual leaders know what is happening in their congregations. Make sure they know you are looking for your next opportunity.

When you network, when you meet with people, whether you know them or not, you cannot sound negative. So if you were fired or laid off, wait a while. Calm yourself. You have to sound positive and optimistic. If you come across as bitter, no one will help you. Attitude is everything. No one wants to help a "Gloomy Gus," because you can't open the door for someone to meet a contact if that person, the contact, will come back and ask, "Why did you send her to me? She has a lousy attitude!" You must have a positive outlook. You got canned. Get over it!

If your job search is not of your own will, be honest with people. It is alright to say you were fired. Tell the truth. Tell what you learned from the experience. It really is that simple. We all make mistakes. Unless you committed a crime, you really don't need to feel ashamed. And if you were laid off, not fired, you certainly have nothing of which to be ashamed.

One question I am always asked is, "How can I contact someone I have not spoken to in years to ask for help? It will sound awful." And they are right. But, they are also wrong.

Remember the LinkedIn connection I referred to earlier who invited me to participate with him on a panel? He was asked that question. His answer was that it did not matter; people will be happy to hear from you. They will not have the "you only are calling because you need something" attitude. They will want to see and help you. The woman who asked the question did not believe him for a minute. But then hands started to rise. Members of the audience told their stories about reaching out to former classmates and colleagues who they had not spoken to, not in years, but in decades. And they were happy to help.

Let's focus on the most common scenario: You are at an event for professionals in your industry. It's a lecture. You take a deep breath, you walk over to a woman who is standing alone looking at the crowd – a sure sign that she too is shy. You both have name tags. So you walk over and introduce yourself: "Hi Mary, I'm Joe. What brings you here?"

Then the most important thing happens because if you do this incorrectly, you can blow it before you even begin. You extend your arm and shake hands. A firm handshake sends a subliminal message of confidence; a weak handshake means you are scared, timid and uncertain. Make certain that when you introduce yourself you make eye contact, smile and give a firm handshake. If you, or the person who you are meeting, does not shake hands for health or religious reasons, just say so. It should not be held against you – or them.

Well, you shook – or rather are shaking – hands. What should Mary say? What should you say? How should this conversation go? Try this:

Hi Mary, I'm Joe. What brings you here?

Hi Joe. I've come to hear the speaker. I'm interested in learning about blockchain. What about you?

Same. So tell me, what do you do for a living?

We shall now pause for a brief commercial message.

This is the point where the elevator pitch is used. Some people will tell you an elevator pitch should be 30-seconds. Some will say 20. They are both wrong. No one wants to hear a stranger talk about themselves for 20, let alone 30, seconds. If you need that much time, you don't know yourself very well! A good elevator pitch takes ten seconds; a great one five.

The purpose of the pitch is simply to get the conversation going. It's a starter, not a finisher.

Put down this book and go to your computer. Open a browser and go to YouTube. Do a search for "TV commercial film for Volkswagen 'Snow Plow'." It is all of 59 seconds. It is generally accepted as the greatest commercial of all time.

As you will see, the commercial begins with the VW Beatle being driven in the snow. At the 27-second mark comes the genius: The announcer asks, "Have you ever wondered how the man who drives the snow plow, drives to the snow plow?" It takes five seconds.

It is not easy to come up with a five-second pitch. But once you have a good 10-second pitch, you will tweak it. With comfort comes speed.

Now let's get back to Joe and Mary:

Well, Joe...

35

Pardon the interruption. The three words people most like to hear are their own name, "you" and "we." Use the person's name. Not only will they give you their undivided attention, but it will make it easier for you to remember their name. (Name tags are usually, but not always, provided at networking events.)

> *... I am the person responsible for keeping teams of 20 to 50 people working efficiently, harmoniously, on time and under budget. What do you do?*

Mary is good. You see, I tricked you. Joe isn't the one looking for the job, Mary is. You don't know what industry she is in. You don't know how long she has been in her current job. You don't know anything about her except for the one thing she wants you to know: what she can do for you, or someone you know, who needs someone who can manage teams. That's a 10-second elevator pitch. Now you have to do the same.

Make it generic. How would you describe what you do to a child? It can be as simple as that. Remember, the elevator pitch is just to start the conversation. It needs to lead to a follow-up question. In the case of Joe, he could ask Mary, "What industry are you in?" "What company do you work for?" Of course, she could have included that information in the pitch but the goal is to have a conversation. Open-ended statements and questions are key.

There are people for whom this is especially difficult. College students immediately come to mind. They should focus on their major. "I am a Computer Science major and I hope to develop apps that will serve non-profits." "I am a History major and I hope to work in Public Relations." "I am a Gender Studies major and I hope my parents don't find out!" (Sorry, I could not resist. "Gender Studies" is what one comedian described as "Majoring in unemployment!" I did a search on LinkedIn for jobs with the keywords "gender studies." In the entire world there were only 879 listed. To be fair, I did the same search for "international relations," my major; there were 7,546. But in all seriousness, doing this type of search on LinkedIn could be a good way to choose a major!)

And then there are veterans. First, thank you for your service. As I understand it, 81% of all jobs in the military have a civilian equivalency. In most cases, therefore, it will be easy: "I'm a Navy veteran. I was a quartermaster and am looking for a position in

Purchasing." Simple. Easy. Straight-forward. But what of the 19% that had a purely military role? That's a little less easy:

"I am a veteran. I was a sergeant in the Infantry. I am looking to get into X."

Notice the three components. First, he said he was a veteran. If the person to whom he is speaking does not respond with, "Thank you for your service," move on! Second, he mentioned his rank. One shocking statistic I read was that only 1 percent of Americans have ever interacted with veterans or active military. Veterans like to talk about "grade" such as "E-6" which, to them, makes sense. The rest of us don't have a clue. So they should only mention rank, not grade. Third, he made it clear the industry in which he is interested, not the *function*. If he had said a specific role it might have narrowed the response. As I said before, open-ended statements and questions.

The Good Lord gave us all an indication regarding how to successfully network. He gave us two ears and one mouth. Listen twice as much as you speak. If you are not listening, you are not learning, and if you are not learning you will not know what you need to do. This brings me to my "Three Knows."

First, and we already dealt with it, you must *know* yourself. Second, you must *know* your audience. That is why you listen twice as much as you speak. You have to find out all you can about them. Let's pursue this further.

You have delivered your pitch and now it is incumbent upon you to find out all you can about your networking partner. While in some foreign countries it may not be appropriate, in the United States it is perfectly acceptable to ask a stranger what they do for a living. And it is also appropriate to ask them about their work. "What do you like about your job?" "How did you get into the field?" "How are you dealing with technology?" I once asked an architect if he considered himself to be an urban planner or an artist. Boy, did that ever get him talking!

Finally, you must *know* what you want. This is no time for Dickens. (*Great Expectations...*) Set your sights low. Make them reasonable. All you want to do is to start the process of building your professional network. You want to meet the right people, the people who can help you.

Of course, the only way to know if they are the *right* people is to start building relationships. And that takes time and effort.

Ironically, or maybe not, your initial conversation only takes a few minutes, unless you discover you really have something in common. So once you know what each of you do, comes the polite, "It was nice meeting you. I hope to see you again." And you walk away. That is not being rude. You are there to meet *people*, plural, not just one person.

The most crucial part of the networking process is follow up, my fifth point. That is where most people fail. Again, networking *is not* exchanging business cards; networking is *building relationships*. When someone gives you their card they are inviting you to contact them. That's why they have them.

You must have a business card. Even if you are unemployed, you have to have a card. It needs to include your name, profession (in the case of students your profession is your major), your phone number, and email address. It is not critical, but you can include your city and state of residence, but I would not advise including your home address.

To continue with our story, you have Mary's contact information. You have the contact information for a number of people. How are you going to remember who said what? You can't, unless you write it down. Now if you met someone and you did not like them, what I do is to bend the corner of their card when I put it in my pocket. When I get home...

Sorry, I need to digress yet again. Keep your cards in one pocket and everyone else's in another. Learn from my mistakes! I once handed a man someone else's card and, after reading it, he smiled and said, "You don't look like a Jane!" He was the one who told me to always place other people's cards in my breast pocket and mine in my side pocket.

And another digression: If you live in a multinational city like New York, you will meet people from many countries and many cultures. There is an art to networking with some people. I already mentioned not offering to shake hands with religious people. For example, observant Jewish men will not shake hands with women and observant women will not shake hands with men. So don't offer. If they put out their hand, by all means, accept the gesture. And then there are Asians. Now technically, just as everyone living in North or South America is an "American," everyone living from Israel to Japan is technically "Asian." But for present purposes I am referring to the Chinese, Japanese and Koreans.

38

When offering or accepting a business card from them you need two hands. Take their card with both hands, look at it, and comment on it. Never write on it! That is a sign of disrespect.

Returning to follow up, at the end of your conversation write on the back of the person's card something key that they told you. Some people laminate their cards. Buy a 99 cent notebook and keep it in your pocket. Again, learn from my mistakes. At the top of the page write the person's name (I didn't and the event was therefore rendered worthless!) and the key thing they told you. (Naturally, this is how you record what the Asians told you.)   Now you can follow-up. Send the following email:

> *Joe,*
>
> *It was a pleasure meeting you yesterday at the whatever event. I hope you found it worthwhile.*
>
> *I especially enjoyed our conversation. I was intrigued when you told me X. With your permission, I will contact you in a few days to see if we can get together to continue our conversation.*
>
> *Thanks in advance.*
>
> *All the best,*
>
> *Mary*

Instead of sending an email, a hand-written note is usually appreciated. Give it a try. My advice is to send emails to "younger" persons, and hand-written notes to "older" persons. For them it may bring back good memories.

A couple of days after you (for present purposes you are "Mary"), send the email, one more for the hand-written note, you call Joe. He agrees to meet with you. You arrive and after the normal pleasantries you get down to business and remind him what he told you. At some point he will ask about your situation and you can tell him, if you have not already done so, that you are looking for your next opportunity. He may ask for a copy of your résumé. And you, naturally, refuse to give it to him!

That's right, you *refuse*. "Sorry, I did not bring a copy. I did not think this was a job interview. As I wrote, I wanted to continue our conversation but, when I get home, I'll be happy to send it to you."

Now you have an excuse to move forward. When you get home you send Joe an email thanking him for meeting with you, which you would have done in any case, but now you can add, "per your request, attached is a copy of my résumé." And you hear nothing from him.

So on a Friday, a week-10 days later, you send him a simple email asking him if, in addition to the résumé that you sent him, there is any other information he would like. You also wish him a good weekend. (That's why you send it on a Friday!) That makes the email sound friendly and not accusatorial – "You asked for my résumé! You never got back to me, you no good so-and-so!" – Maybe he never received it. Maybe he did but forgot about it. Maybe he did but never intended to do anything with it. Or maybe...

Ten minutes after you send the email Joe calls you. He's furious. "Didn't you hear from Mark?" he asks. "No," you reply. "Who's Mark?"

Well, it turns out Mark is the person to whom he sent your résumé. And now Joe is upset that Mark did not follow-up with you. So he calls Mark and Mark apologies and promises to call you right away, which he does.

You speak with Mark and then what do you do? You follow-up with Joe and let him know that you have scheduled a meeting with Mark on Tuesday and you thank him for having made the connection.

At the meeting Mark tells you to contact Sally. When you get home you send an email to Joe telling him that Mark was helpful and that he referred you to one of his contacts (he does not have to know who). Then you contact Sally. For sake of argument, you reach her right away and you set up an appointment with her. You then write to Mark, thank him for the meeting and the introduction, and update him.

After you meet with Sally, you tell Mark what happened. Joe need not be informed. And, of course, you thank Sally.

The key is to keep everyone in the loop so that they know that you follow-through. If you do not, they will think you are a waste of their time. That is the one thing you cannot afford. So follow-up and follow-through.

And this entire process, where you ended up with not one but numerous new contacts, all began with a three to five minute chat at a networking or other professional event. That is the definition of time well-spent.

Remember, when you ask for what is called an "informational" meeting, the first meeting between Mary and Joe, you do not bring your résumé. You will not need to bring your résumé to the subsequent meetings because the second and third people you meet, in this case Mark and Sally, should already have copies. That said, it can't hurt to have a couple of hard copies with you. (It's the same when you have a job interview. Too often people tell me that the interviewer(s) could not find their résumés!)

While not strictly a part of networking, and even though, as stated, the vast majority of jobs are not advertised, don't ignore job boards like ZipRecruiter, Indeed and Idealist. As long as they don't charge you for using their sites, use them. And go old school as well; check out the classified listings in your local newspapers or on their websites.

There is also no reason not to share your résumé with recruiters. The more the merrier. I'll tell you now, they will never respond. (I will! Email me your résumé to bh@hsstaffing.com.) Recruiters do not work for you, they work for their clients. So they will only contact you if they need you. If they are not working on a search which requires someone with your qualifications, you will not hear from them. That's the reality of working with recruiters.

Whatever you do, do not call recruiters to badger them. They don't like it. When a recruiter does work *with* you *for* one of their clients, by all means follow-up with them especially after you get an interview with the client. Get feedback. Be certain to thank them. It's rare, so it should be appreciated. But you most certainly, after you meet with their client, the employer, may contact the employer directly. In fact, you must. As we will discuss when we review interviewing, you *have to* send the employer, the people who interview you, a thank-you email. You *should* send one to the recruiter as well. A simple "thank you for arranging the interview," will suffice.

Volunteering. A great way to expand your network is volunteering. But only volunteer for a cause in which you truly believe. And insist on their taking advantage of your skills. That is what you have to contribute: your professional knowledge. The goal is to be sitting around the table, literally, with people who will eventually be able to help you. You want the right people to see the quality of your work. When asked why you decided to volunteer, just say, "I am between jobs and now have time to give back." If you say that you hope to get a job, you figuratively just shot yourself in the foot!

The beauty of volunteering is not just that it will allow you to be with the right people, it will also get you out of your own head. It will give you something meaningful to do. Oh, and you will also be helping people in need or an important cause.

Lastly, and of special importance for college students, school-time jobs and internships will not only help you have an impressive résumé, they will also either (a) result in a permanent job, or (b) in a referral or reference that will get you a job. It's all part of networking.

Reading

Finally, your entire job search, sooner or later, will involve interacting with people. One day it may be Watson and his offspring (clones?), but not today and not tomorrow. So you have to be an interesting person.

The more you read, the better. At networking events and interviews, things will come up. The best way to be prepared is to be knowledgeable. You don't need to be an expert, you just need to be interesting and appear smart. This will especially help you when you are surprised by a question someone asks you, especially in an interview. Also, if the person who is talking to you thinks you are bored, having a question to ask, even one that shows your ignorance, will save the situation, because being interested in what someone is saying is more important than being knowledgeable about the topic. Asking questions is a great way to compliment someone and to let them know that you are aware of, and not ashamed of, your limitations.

One candidate I had for an executive recruiting client was totally derailed, even though the interview had been going well, when, out of left field, the CEO asked her, "What was the last movie you saw?"

Now it is true that there are ulterior motives behind some questions. The best example is, "What is your biggest weakness?" They are really asking, "Why shouldn't we hire you?" But, as they say, "Sometimes a cigar is just a cigar." Sometimes a question is just a question. The ulterior motive is to get to know you.

Interviewers ask surprise questions all the time. Don't become flustered. Take a few seconds to think about a response. If you practiced, that is the same as training, and, as everyone knows, when you let your training "kick in," when you have faith in what you have learned, things usually turn out alright. Practice, really does, make perfect.

But my client could not remember the last movie she saw and became totally flustered.

If I may be permitted, I would have said that I have not seen a movie in years. I read books. I would have changed the subject to books.

Once, at a networking event, I met an oenophile. I don't like, drink or know anything at all about wine. But that was all the man wanted to talk about. He owned a company, not related to wine, and I had been told he was looking to hire. I wanted him as an executive recruiting client. So I told him I knew nothing about wine, but I did know about rare books and first editions. I told him that first editions are more valuable when their dustcovers are in perfect condition. I asked him if in fact, he did not collect wine, or bottles, but rather the labels on the bottles. He was thrilled! And I got what I wanted, a meeting. That was my goal. When I network, I take everything one step at a time. First a meeting; then a contract.

Of course, eventually, you will, either through networking or responding to ads, have the opportunity to apply for a job. To that, we now turn our attention.

Part Two: Applying

Before you start applying for jobs you have to make certain you are a viable candidate, generally speaking, for any position you may want. This pertains mainly to persons starting out or changing careers. Let's consider both separately, although there are commonalities.

College students, for example, must show that they are work-focused and not play-focused. If all they did in college was go to class, they made a big mistake. Employers, as noted, want to see internships and jobs on a résumé. They need to know that the college student understands what it means to actually have a job and put in a full day's work. (In fact, one employer I know will only hire people who had jobs during high school!)

Also, and this is for everyone, study English. I don't care what your major is; English should be your minor. The only way to advance in a job (at least in the US) is to speak and write well in English. If you can't do it, you will reach a plateau in your career and advancement will elude you.

Persons changing careers must have the knowledge required for their new career. This may entail going back to school to learn, for example, the latest software. How is it possible to know what employers in a new career want? Simple. Look at the "Qualifications" section of job descriptions, a subject we will be discussing in detail. It's all right there!

I once had an "older" woman come to me for career counseling. For some 30 years she had worked as a secretary (for her, that was not a bad word; she was proud of it!) for a lawyer who had decided to close his practice. She had great skills that rarely exist today: Short-hand and dictation come to mind. And she knew Word Perfect, in my opinion, the best word processing software of all time. Problem was, today, only lawyers use it. (I used it to write my doctorate, in the late 1980s, when it was popular in academia.) She did not know Word or any Microsoft products. When I told her not to bother looking for work until she learned Word, Excel and Outlook, she admitted that others had told her the same. I ran into her a couple of weeks after our first session. She decided to retire rather than go back to school. That may have been the right decision for her; it may not be for you!

But there is one final note, especially for immigrants. I lived in Israel for 13 years. I had to learn Hebrew. Technically, I was fluent, but in reality, I was pretty to very good, depending on the conversation. I could understand better than I could speak. And I had an "American" accent. But I could hear it and, therefore, was usually able to control it. Even when I could not, I was still understandable albeit in an unpleasant tone of voice. (Verbal nails on a blackboard!) I understand the sensitivity of what I am about to write.

If you have a heavy accent, if it is difficult for Americans to understand you, on the phone or in-person, you *must* seek professional help. It is called "accent reduction." It is nothing of which to be ashamed. But let me make this clear, if an employer does not hire you because of your accent, it is *not* discrimination. Even if it is not written in the job description, and it won't be, you have to speak in such a way that colleagues, customers, clients, vendors and everyone else concerned with the business will be able to understand. That's a given. This is on you and no one else.

What is also on you is organizing your job search. That means keeping track of what you are doing. The downside is that after a while you will have a list of hundreds of places to which you have applied with, possibly, only modest results. Do not forget that a job search is a numbers game; the more applications, the better your chances. *The phone will ring.*

When it does, you need to know for what position you applied. It is not the end of the world if you have to ask the caller, but it is best if you do not. The phone rings and the caller says, "I am calling from XYZ about your application." A considerate caller will add, "for the BLANK position." But it does not always happen. So you need a record. You need a record for another, perhaps more important, reason. You do not want to apply to the same place for the same job. It will happen; it always does. If the applications were sent months apart, not a big deal. Days apart? Big deal.

This is very simple to deal with this. Create an Excel spreadsheet. In the first cell insert the name of the company. Proceeding horizontally, in the second cell insert the position, then the date you applied, who you sent it to, then their email, phone number, and, lastly, their website. If you should enter the name of the company a second time, let's say weeks later, Excel should – it does not always happen – autopopulate the cell in column A where you entered the company name, since you had done so previously in the same column. Then you can check to see when you applied and for which position.

Applying for different positions in the same company is not a very good idea. If you are applying for totally different positions, it will appear that you do not know what you want or what you have to offer. If you apply for similar positions, that may be interpreted as a lack of confidence: "She applied for the director and the assistant director position. Does that mean she does not think she is good enough for the directorship or that she will settle for the assistant directorship?" See? So if there are multiple positions in the same department, apply for the position that you objectively feel you are most qualified for and let the HR Department decide if they want to consider you for something else. It happens all the time.

This brings up another issue: What if you see the job description, our next topic, and realize that you really are not qualified, but still want to work for the company? Simple. Pretend that you don't know about the job. Send an email to the company's HR Department introducing yourself. It should be personalized to the HR director. The second paragraph should highlight what you consider to be the greatest success in your career. In a perfect world, it should relate to the job you saw advertised. Let HR decide if you are qualified. If you apply for the advertised position, and are clearly not qualified, they will be frustrated and think that you can't read! So let *them* consider you. Write something like this which is similar to the email I suggested when discussing researching:

Subject: Introduction

Ms. Jane Smith
Director, Human Resources
XYZ Corporation
123 Main Street
Anytown, ST 12345

Dear Ms. Smith,

I wish to take this opportunity to introduce myself in the hope that you will consider me if a position opens at XYZ which matches my qualifications.

Over the past ten years I have saved my employer millions of dollars by streamlining our acquisition process and revamping our accounting systems to uncover attempted fraud and waste. I look forward to doing the same for you.

Attached please find a copy of my résumé for your review.

Thank you in advance for your consideration.

Sincerely,

John Doe
123-456-7890

Job Descriptions

Good job descriptions, and sadly there are not many, have four sections:

The first section is the company description. Read it! Go to their website and see if it feels like something of which you would like to be a part, or, for that matter, apart! The second section should be the "Requirements" for the position. Is that the work you want to be doing day in and day out? The third section should be "Qualifications." We'll get back to that in a minute. The final section should explain the Compensation package. In some jurisdictions, it is illegal for an employer to ask a candidate what they earned in the past or are earning currently. It is to eliminate the gender pay gap. More on that in Part Four. But for now, what is important is that many employers will reveal the salary range upfront in the job description, along with the benefits. Again, we'll get into this in more detail in Part Four, but the question you have to ask yourself is simple, Does the salary meet your needs?

Returning to "Qualifications," the not so simple question is, Are you qualified? And this is where most people fail.

I would not even hazard to guess how many people have come to me for career counseling totally frustrated by the fact that they were not getting any responses to their applications, let alone interviews. I would ask to see the job descriptions for the positions for which they had applied. Nine times out of ten, they were not qualified. And when I told them, they always responded, "But I can do it. It's perfect for me!" And that is the problem.

The number one mistake job seekers make is that they are focused on themselves. Remember? I told you that earlier. When you read the "Qualifications" section of the job description, you have to read it from the perspective of *the employer*. It is what *the employer* needs that counts, *not* what *you* want. If you can't meet *their* needs, if you can't solve the problem for which they are looking to hire someone, they are not going to be interested in you. Period. End of sentence. End of discussion.

But only in part. As I just explained, if you are unqualified for the job, either over- or under qualified, you at least know that the company is hiring. So send them the letter on the previous page.

That letter is the equivalent of a "cold call," meaning you don't know the person and they do not know you. But there is a "warm call," or, for our purposes, a "warm" introductory letter. This is when someone suggests that you contact the company. In this case you begin the letter with, "I am writing at the suggestion of..." That way you are more likely to get a response. And, if you don't, you can contact the person who suggested you write, tell them that you did not hear back from the person to whom they suggested you send the email, and ask their advice. They may have a vested interest, in fact, it will be a matter of personal pride, to find out why their name did not open a figurative (and maybe even a literal) door for you.

But when it is not *who* you know, but *what* you know, "Qualifications" is key. So how do you read it?

First, the order of the qualifications is usually most important. If you don't meet the first requirement, or at least two of the first three, move on. Second, pay attention to the wording. "Must have" means you have to have it; "preferred" means, it would be nice but, if you have everything else, or most everything else, or maybe something we had not considered, we'll take a look at you.

We will be dealing with *illegal* discrimination later, but for now let's look at *legal* discrimination:

Under "Qualifications" you will find some, or all, of the following: Minimum number of years of experience; college degree; ability to stand for long periods or lift a minimum amount of weight; have a current license or certification. No, this is not age discrimination, racial or socio-economic discrimination, discrimination against the disabled, or discrimination of any kind. Companies have the right to decide what they need in a candidate for a specific position. Sometimes, in the case of licenses and certifications, it's the law. In this hypothetical case, they need someone who already knows the job, writ large, who will not require micromanagement. They need someone with a college degree so that they know that they can finish a major project, will fit in with their staff, all of whom have degrees, and will get along with clients, almost all of whom have degrees. They need someone who will be able to literally pull their own weight, perhaps stand for long hours at trade shows and help to setup and dismantle displays. And they need someone who can legally hold the position. These requirements are all perfectly legitimate, reasonable and lawful.

My favorite example is obesity. I have researched it and there are very good cases to me made for or against being able to discriminate against someone on the basis of their weight or size. There is a term of which you should be aware, *bona fide occupational qualification*. It means what it says. Here's the example: Do you really want an obese person, regardless of their qualifications and abilities, as a flight attendant on an airplane on which you are flying? Sometimes the qualification has to take precedence over an individual's rights.

The most important qualification for deciding whether or not to apply for a job is years of experience. The rest is straight forward. Either you have the degree or you don't. Either you have the specific experience required for the job, or you don't. Either you have the degree, license or certification, or you don't. But years of experience is hard.

Generally speaking, if an employer does not include years of experience as a requirement, it is probably an entry-level position. You should be able to figure that out from the other qualifications. If "one to three years" is a requirement, and you have four or five, go for it. But if you have ten or more years, you are wasting your time, as will someone applying for a job for which they only have a couple of years of experience when the requirement is for ten or more. (For college students, *serious* projects which you successfully completed, may be counted as one year's experience.)

I have worked on two searches that speak to this subject. The first was an IT position. Young candidates complained that they were being discriminated against because they did not have as much experience as the older candidates who they assumed, they did not know, were being considered, and older candidates thought they were being discriminated against because they had too much experience. The truth was, there were two finalists, one probably in his mid-twenties and the other, probably in his late-fifties, early-sixties. They offered the job first to the "young" guy but his references were lousy. The "old" guy got the job.

And then there was an administrative search on which I was working. It was rather amusing. My client rejected everyone and never filled the position. The white candidates complained they were discriminated against because they were not black or Hispanic. The black and Hispanic candidates complained that they were being discriminated against because they were not white. The women, because they were not men. The men, because they were not women. The young because they were not old enough, and the old because they were not young enough. I laughed and told them the truth which, of course, they refused to believe. Sometimes everyone is rejected and sometimes it's because the employer does not have their act together. Remember that!

I'll come back to this but, for now, the important thing is that you don't use discrimination as your default excuse for not getting an interview or an offer. Employers are not looking to be sued; they are looking for the best candidates. Yes, there is discrimination in the world, but you'll never be able to prove it. And if you default to discrimination, you will be denying yourself the ability to improve. You won't even consider that the fault may be your own. I'll give you one example:

A gentleman came to me in his late-forties early-fifties distraught because he was not getting any job offers, convinced he was being discriminated against. The problem was not with his cover letter or résumé since he was having, on average, at least one interview a week. Clearly he was doing something wrong in the interview and, after doing mock interviews for an hour and a half, I could not figure out what it was. He was a master!

Then I decided to ask the "easy" questions which I had ignored given how skilled he was. The first question I asked him was, "What are your weaknesses?" He replied, "Procrastination." That was all he said. That was all he told me and that was all he had told interviewers.

"Why," I asked, "would anyone want to hire a procrastinator?" It turned out he never explained how he overcame his procrastination. Once he let interviewers know what he did so that he did not miss deadlines, he got a job offer.

Sometimes it is important to step back and look at yourself critically and unemotionally. It is very difficult to do. If you don't have true friends, friends who will tell you what you may not want to hear, friends who can be brutally honest, then you should consider hiring a professional. Just make certain that they have actually hired and fired people. I have been on many panels with career counselors. It is very easy to tell which ones have experience in the work place and which have experience reading books about conducting successful job searches. Don't hire an academic; hire someone with real experience!

Once you have determined that you believe the employer will believe that you meet the minimum qualifications for the job, it is time to apply. I am regularly asked how to apply for jobs online. In other words, how to fill out the form. My answer is simple: Do what they tell you to do. If it is "required," do it! But there are two exceptions:

First, and I have done, or rather not done, this myself. NEVER give out your Social Security Number. Unless you are applying for a government position, no employer needs to know your SSN prior to making you a conditional offer of employment. More on this in Part Four.

Second, don't give out the names of references until there is mutual interest in the job. Again, more on this in Part Four.

Whether online or by email, you may need a cover letter and will need a résumé.

The Ten-Second Cover Letter

An interesting question is what to do if an employer does *not* request a cover letter. Should you include one?

It's a judgment call. If you don't include one, it will not be held against you. If you do include one, the employer may think that you always do more than you are asked and that could be held against you. On the other hand, if you include one and show that you write well, understand business, can prioritize and get to the point, that may be to your advantage.

If you are applying online, you may have a choice. If you are applying via email, there really is none. You have to write something in your email! You just can't attach a résumé although, truth be told, I have received blank emails from applicants who I never submitted to my client(s)... So what do you write in that email? It will be your cover letter.

A cover letter has to be short, sweet and to the point. Why? Because for an advertised position, depending on the industry, an employer can receive scores, if not hundreds, of applications. In fact, I went to a presentation for an IT company and their representative said that they receive *thousands* of applications every time they post a job! Do the math: If it takes 2 minutes to read a cover letter, how much time will the Human Resources Department need to spend reading cover letters? Do you really think they are going to spend hours? A 2-minute letter is too long. It sends the message that you cannot prioritize. You do not know what is important. In meetings you will talk too much! *Ten seconds* is the perfect length.

There is another reason why you want to keep the letter brief. If you are writing too much, just as if you talk too much, there is more opportunity for misunderstanding. The bottom line is, it does not matter what you write, what matters is what the recipient *reads*. And if they read something that you did not intend to write...

So what do you write?

Even though this is an email, it still needs to be written like a professional letter, using proper English. Sadly, people – including some college graduates! – don't know how to write letters. That's actually a good thing for you because the bar has been set very low. Write a good letter and you have already positively differentiated yourself from your competition.

The truth is, you will not always know to which company you are applying. In order to avoid applicants calling to find out if their applications have been received, some companies do not give their names. They want applications sent to a Gmail or other free-service account.

Which reminds me, never follow-up with an HR Department. They do not like it. If you are calling to see if they received your résumé, that means they are on the phone and not actually processing the résumés. It's their job to process résumés, not talk to applicants until they decide to do so. Don't call them! They got your résumé. They will call you when and if they are ready.

If you know the name of the company, include it. If not, well, you can't. The same thing goes for the name of the person to whom you are submitting the résumé. If at all possible, try to find out who the person is, but do not call HR; try the company's main line. But first, go to their website or their LinkedIn page. You might even find it on Facebook. Sometimes simply Googling "Human Resources Director at X" will get you the name. (If that does not work, try "Vice President of... .")

If you can't find the name, "Dear Hiring Manager" will suffice. Don't use "Dear Sir or Madame," that's old school, and "To Whom it May Concern," well, that just makes it sound like a form letter. And you never want to appear to be sending a form letter.

The goal of a cover letter is to get the recipient to look at your résumé. That's it. The goal is not to get an interview. That's the goal, or purpose, of the résumé. So what should you do?

In the "Subject" line of the email, write the name of the position, and if there is one, the code.

Next, tell them why you are writing. That way they know you can get to the point and respect their time. After all, they could be trying to fill multiple positions. They will appreciate it. Then, tell them where you saw the ad. Now they know that you understand business. It is important for them to know where they are getting the best return on their advertising dollars. You are helping them. They will appreciate that as well.

Now give them one really good reason why they should consider you for the position. Think of the cover letter as though it were a movie trailer. It is a tease, not to get them into a theatre, but to literally turn the page and look at your résumé.

Then reference your résumé and end with a polite close. And that is all there is to it. You now have an effective cover letter that can be read in ten seconds.

Here is an example. If you are presently employed, after the word "apply" write "in confidence" so that they know not to contact your present employer which, to be totally honest, is very rare.

Subject: Controller Position (No. 1234)

Ms. Jane Smith
Director, Human Resources
XYZ Corporation
123 Main Street
Anytown, ST 12345

Dear Ms. Smith,

Applying

I wish to apply for the Controller position which I saw posted on Indeed.com.

Over the past ten years, I have saved my employer millions of dollars by streamlining our acquisition process and revamping our accounting systems to uncover attempted fraud and waste.

Attached please find a copy of my résumé for your review.

Thank you in advance for your consideration. I look forward to hearing from you.

Sincerely,

John Doe
123-456-7890

You decided on the focus of the key paragraph, the second paragraph, based on the job description. It was clear that the company's main interest was in reducing costs and waste. So you let them know that you have a track record of doing just that. No self-praise, which many people advice to include. The logic is for you to tell the employer that you can solve their problem. The logic is not to tell the employer how great you think you are.

News flash! Employers do not care what you think about yourself. Obviously, if you are going to write anything, you will write positive things. So it is meaningless. The only thing they want to know is that you can do the job. And the simplest way to convince them of that is to tell them that you have already done it.

The rest is self-explanatory.

You now have your cover letter. It only took you minutes to write, and seconds to be read. And if it is effective, and I believe it will be, your résumé will then come into play.

The Five-Second Résumé

You have worked very hard on your résumé. You may have spent days, if not weeks, on it. You may have actually paid someone good money to write it for you. You may have read countless articles offering contradictory advice. Well, you will be happy to know that you can stop reading. This is how you write an effective résumé, meaning, a résumé that will get you an interview. Let's begin in the weeds, so to speak:

The margins of the first page should be half an inch at the top, and an inch at the bottom and sides. All additional pages (and, no, a résumé does not have to be limited to one page, it needs to be as long as it needs to be to accurately represent what you have to offer) should have one inch margins all around. As a header or footer, your choice, starting on the second page, your name and the page number should appear.

But let's talk about a bit more about the aesthetics of the résumé. Keep it clean and neat. Unless you are applying for a job as a graphic designer, shaded boxes, infographics, and colored fonts (other than black) are a waste and can be self-defeating. Many companies, especially major corporations, scan résumés. All of the aforementioned nonsense can ruin the scan. You want racial harmony: Black letters on a white background. By all means put some things in bold and italics. I would suggest your name, the name of your employers and the dates of employment in bold, and a blurb about the employer in italics. And use a 12-point font. If, in order to not have the last page of your résumé consist of only one or two lines you have to use an 11-point font, so be it. But if the recipient of the résumé can't read it, because the font is too small, it won't be read.

Begin your résumé, at the top of the first page, with your **name** and any legitimate designation you have: CPA, PMP, PhD, etc. (in 14-point font for style). If you have an androgynous name, or a foreign (to the United States) name, place "Ms." or "Mr." in front of your first name. This has nothing to do with anything other than being polite and showing that you are anticipating a very natural and human question, "Is this person a woman or a man?" If you think they are going to discriminate against you because of your gender, don't worry, they could discriminate against you just as easily because of what they guess is your nationality or religion. Don't worry about it. Be considerate. In any event, do you really want to work for a bigot, a racist, a misogynist, or a misandrist?

There is something else people with a foreign name should consider. I have advised clients to write in parenthesis after their name, in italics, the transliteration so the recipient will know how to pronounce it. This also shows that you are a considerate person.

Obviously the recipient of the résumé is going to ask themselves how to pronounce your name. So tell them! They'll appreciate it.

I suggest centering your name and, underneath, insert your **city and state of residence**. No one needs to know your street address. All an employer needs to know is where you live. This is important because they may want someone local (in which case it should be stated on the job description) or within a reasonable commuting distance. (That's also legal discrimination!) After that should come your personal **phone number**, not your work number and, to save space, on the same line should be your **email** address. Under that include the full **URL**s for your LinkedIn Profile and any online work portfolios you may have.

You have to be contactable. If you use your work number, well, you are looking for a job, aren't you? Recruiters and employers keep résumés on file. Hopefully, you will not be with your current employer much longer. So how is a prospective employer, in the future, going to find you? Moreover, don't include you work number if you don't want to be called at work!

While it is not as prevalent now as it once was, make certain your email address isn't stupid. I once refused to submit a résumé from a young woman whose email address was "daddyslittleprincess@example.com." There and then, in my office, I made her get a Gmail account. Keep it professional.

Which brings me back to your phone. Make certain your voice mail is working. If you can't be reached because your voice mail has not been set up or, for that matter, if your box is full, whoever is calling you may not call back. If they reach another applicant, you may be out of luck. And then there is your voice mail message. Foolishness is a turn off. I only know of one exception.

I once dialed a number of a candidate for a fundraising position. The recording I heard went something like, "Thanks for calling. You have reach Flubo the Clown. After the tone, leave your message and I'll get back to you as soon as I can." And it was followed by a clown laugh and horn honk. I called back just to make certain I had dialed the correct number. I had and I left a message.

"Flubo" called me back. His résumé was good. He sounded normal on the phone. And I got his permission to submit his résumé to my client. And then I told him to change his phone message, replacing "Flubo the Clown" with his actual name. He refused. He explained that on weekends he volunteered at local hospitals as "Flubo the Clown."

I submitted him and when I called my client to see what they thought of his résumé, they told me it was solid but he did not appear to be a star. Then I suggested that they call him but I warned them about the phone message. It was the message, or the fact that he volunteered at hospitals, that got him the interview. (We'll get to volunteering shortly, but for now, suffice it to note that he did not have his volunteer activities on his résumé because he did not consider them "work related." He was wrong. Don't make that mistake.)

In any event, you are not Flubo. Keep your message professional.

Now is the time to tell you a secret which, when I published it on LinkedIn, a lot of people were angry about. Your résumé is not going to be *read*. Your résumé is going to be *skimmed*. It takes five seconds. When I, and any other professional, receives a résumé, all we do is look to see where the person lives, how long they have remained on their jobs, and if they have the necessary skills, licenses, certifications or degrees to be considered for the position. That's it. If I need local and you are not local, you get filed. If I need a CPA and you are not a CPA, you get filed. If I need someone with a security license and you don't have one, you get filed. If I need someone with a graduate degree in Computer Science, and you don't have one, you get filed. It's that simple. And that's why I call it "the five-second résumé."

Before continuing, it is important to consider "jumpers," people who stay at their jobs for less than two years. If there is a pattern, there is a problem. Employers will immediately assume that the individual is not worth the investment in their training. But it depends on the reasons and they won't ask, so you have to tell them, preferably in the résumé, because you want to keep the cover letter short.

If, as I have heard numerous times, the candidate says that their bosses were always out to get them, the candidate has a serious attitude problem and may need professional help. Once, maybe. Twice, possibly. But three or more times? No one has that much bad luck.

If the reason is because the person has been trapped in contract positions, the so-called "gig economy," and wants to get out of it, then, and I know I am getting ahead of myself, on the résumé all of the jobs should be listed under "Contract Work," with the dates of all the jobs combined, followed by a list of the clients and a very brief description of the assignments. But beware! Many employers will not hire consultants. They are concerned that the person will not know how to work in an office, or that they are interested in stealing clients to build their own business and getting training to open their own (competing) business. These are legitimate concerns so keep them in mind if you are thinking about working for yourself before you have worked for someone else.

To return to the five-second résumé skim, there is a simple way to change it into a 10-second skim. Simply provide the reader with something short and interesting to read.

After your name and contact information should NOT come "Objective." Your objective is to get the job for which you are applying. If it is not, don't apply. If you write something in the "Objective" that is not a perfect match for the position, the recipient will think you are not interested. If it is exactly the same as the position, they will think that you change it for every job for which you apply and it will have no legitimacy. There is no reason to have an "Objective" on the résumé.

Similarly, a "Professional Summary," or "Professional Statement," is a total waste of space. Again, as I said before, no one cares what you think of yourself. The only thing an employer wants to know is if you can solve their problem. That is why they are hiring; they have a problem. Show them you are the solution.

Additionally, do not include your photo or any personal information on your résumé, including your Social Security number, date of birth, marital status, and names and ages of your children. That may be acceptable in some foreign countries; it is not acceptable in the United States. (By all means, if you are foreign-born, include "Authorized to work in the United States" on the résumé.)

To stop the five-second skim, your résumé should begin, front and center, with **Selected Accomplishments**. This takes me back to my previous comment about the length of a résumé.

Think about this: A young person, fresh out of college, has a two-page résumé. Why? Because they have already done something with their lives: Real jobs, real internships, volunteering. Compared to a one-pager, it's impressive.

Think about this: An older person, with 10 or 15 years of experience has a one-page résumé. Fifteen years of work that can be summarized on one eight and a half by 11 sheet of paper? Not very impressive, is it?

Let's get back to Selected Accomplishments. It needs to be impressive because it is this section that will turn the five-second skim into a 10-second skim and, more importantly, into an actual *read* that may convince the reader that you are worth a phone call even if you lack some of the things that they (think) they really want or need.

All you need is half a dozen bullet points. And if you can quantify things, so much the better. Remember what I said earlier? The purpose of the cover letter is to get the recipient to look at the résumé. So you already have your first bullet point, the second paragraph of your cover letter, summarized, as it is now a bullet point and no longer a paragraph.

Here are two examples:

- Increased sales an average of 25% each year, over a 5-year period, resulting in added revenue in excess of $10 million.
- Successfully managed 9 union elections.

Just so you understand, and obviously the first is self-explanatory, the second was for a vice president of Human Resources position at a nursing home. It meant that he had kept the union out of his home *nine times*.

In both cases, and these are real examples, those first bullet points were all my clients cared about. Both candidates got interviews.

Allow me to digress for a moment and deal with veterans.

A veteran whose job in the military had no civilian equivalency has to focus on the skills that made them successful in their job. The best example I can give was a résumé I received from a sniper. It was rather amusing. His résumé read as though he was looking for a job as a sniper. There aren't any snipers in the civilian world!

We worked on the résumé and simply listed the skills he needed, the attributes he had, that made him a good sniper. (Of course, we never mentioned any of the "statistical results" of his success.) So employers read under "Selected Accomplishments,"

- Highly decorated veteran of the US Marine Corps
- Known for focus, patience, calmness under stress
- Led team of Marines in extremely dangerous situations with no loss of life

Let's return to the résumé structure.

After Selected Accomplishments comes **Skills**. To save space, if you can, list them in three columns. Don't do what some very foolish people do, and list every "keyword" associated with a profession. If you list a computer language, for example, and you really don't know it, that's called lying and your résumé will be flagged. How will you feel if, in the interview, they ask you about X and you have to admit that you really don't know it? What do you think they will do? Never lie on a résumé. If you get the job, and get caught, you can be fired. Don't lie! And make certain to include any languages that you speak other than English, if you are a native English speaker. Foreign languages can open up new opportunities for employers and make bi- or multi-lingual candidates very attractive.

Next comes **Work Experience**. Obviously, here is where you list where you have worked and your key responsibilities. But let's sort of digress and discuss the feared "résumé gap."

You have been unemployed for a long time. What do you do? Well, my suggestion is, insert the sub-heading, "Employment-Related Activities" and give the dates as from the date of your last job "to present." This is your opportunity to show a prospective employer that you are not the type of person who can remain idle. You are taking advantage of your unemployment. You are staying current and becoming a better candidate/employee. So what should you list?

Classes that you have taken. It does not matter if they are at a school or online, what matters is what you have learned. You did it for the knowledge, not a piece of paper. That said, if you received a certification or license, list them! Include any part-time or contract jobs, even if not related to your profession. These show that you can leave your ego at the door and do what you have to do to support yourself and your family. Finally, your current volunteer activities. Employers like prospects who volunteer. It shows character. More on volunteering later.   (Just to be clear, once you obtain employment, all of these will be transferred to the relevant sections of the résumé.)

Two "non-jobs" about which I am passionate and really aggravate me when I hear that people were advised not to include them on their résumés, are Stay-at-home Parent and Caregiver.

Raising children, keeping a home functioning, is a *real* job. I think it was Teddy Roosevelt, in his autobiography, who wrote that it was the most important job! Think of all the things you learned: Budgeting; scheduling; navigating government bureaucracies; leadership; prioritization; and patience. I would really like to see as a first Selected Accomplishments, "Raised three children, all of whom made the Dean's List and all of whom are attending college." What? That's not a real success? An employer would not be impressed? Be serious!

As for Caregiver, taking care of a loved-one, especially someone with Alzheimer's, is as difficult as it is noble, and it is most certainly a *real* job. I used to work at non-profits helping seniors, including two nursing homes. Pardon my language, but the only way to accurately describe being a caregiver for someone with Alzheimer's is "hell." It is terrible. And once you are done, you have many of the skills of the Stay-at-home Parent, and then some.

In both cases, I have successfully recommended that these heroes apply for Customer Service jobs. In Customer Service, you have to be able to control your temper, communicate clearly, and be patient. What employer in need of Customer Service staff would not want someone with these experiences?

One other note: In both of these cases a message is being sent. In the first, my kids are grown; you have nothing to worry about. In the second, sadly, my loved-one has passed; I am free. You, Employer, do not have to worry that I will have to deal with family issues.

How do you list your places of employment? You begin with the most recent and work your way backwards. How far back should you go? I recommend 15 years. It is hard to be precise since dates of employment cannot be altered. That would be lying. So if, for sake of argument, between 12 and 18 years ago you were employed at the same place, you would have to go back 18 years. If, prior to 18 years you worked at some impressive places, you can, after you have finished listing your most recent jobs, have a subheading, "Previous Employment," and just include the names of the employers, their locations, your titles, and years of employment. But for the main section of Work Experience, include the following:

On the first line, in bold, put the name of the employer; their location; and the dates (years are good enough; months and years are fine) you were employed. Some people are uncomfortable giving the name of their current employer, so instead they write, "Confidential." In that case, the first question they will be asked is, "Where do you work?" If they refuse to answer, the interview will end before it begins. Don't play games. As noted above, add in the cover letter that you are submitting your résumé "in confidence." If you want, you can write "Confidential" at the top of the résumé. But one way or another, you are going to have to reveal where you work. My advice is to do it up front.

The location is important because the recipient may be concerned about a commute. I had one candidate, for a client in Manhattan, who lived in Philadelphia. All of her jobs had been in Manhattan. Every morning she took the train into the City, and every evening she took the train home. That's an hour and a half train ride, one way, *if all goes well*, plus however long it takes to get from Penn Station to work. And on top of that, she lived outside of Philadelphia, so it could have been a five-hour commute every day. And she had been doing it for some 20 years! So I had no concerns that she did not realize, or appreciate, what the commute would be like. Others, on the other hand, do not understand what their commute would be. That is why I always suggest that my clients interview candidates first thing in the morning.

Dates of employment are, as already noted, critical. "Jumpers" need not apply! Now I will tell you a secret: People don't read résumés, especially when they are skimming them. After a while, all résumés begin to look alike. We miss things. Don't make us work. If you were employed at the same company for a long time, and had a number of promotions, put the overall years parallel to the name and location of the company, and next to each title, in brackets, indicate the years for that specific job. That way, the recipient won't get confused and think that you had five jobs in 10 years, instead of one.

Next, in italics, write a brief two- or three-line blurb about the company; and then, on a new line, bullet points showing your *main* responsibilities. Let's consider each separately.

A short blurb shows that you can write. Second, even if it is a well-known company, you did not work for the entire company, you worked for one department. Describe it. Explain what the department/company does (or did, as the case may be), and give some indication of size. Be careful not to disclose any proprietary information.

Following that, comes your title. A lot of people like to change their titles, thinking it does not matter. It does. Even if you were a "coordinator," and everyone else with your job was a "director," stick with "coordinator." Never lie on a résumé. No employer in their right mind will be impressed by a title; they are impressed by what a person actually accomplished and for what they were responsible.

Finally, bullet points of your key responsibilities. Always use bullets because they are easier to read. This allows you to show that you can prioritize your responsibilities. I once had a director come to me for résumé help. He had included "Correspondence" under his responsibilities. Not good.

This is how it should look:

XYZ Incorporated, New York, NY 2010-Present
XYZ is the industry leader in the manufacture of widgets. With operations across the United States and in 15 foreign countries, XYZ has revenues from 17 product lines exceeding $1 billion.

Vice President, Finance (2015-Present)
Assistant VP, Finance (2010-2015)

- Budget forecasting
- Oversight of acquisitions

You get the idea. And notice the blank lines between the sections. You should do everything you can to make the document easy to read.

Following Work Experience comes **Education**, unless you are straight out of college, with no work experience. In that case Education will go first and, unlike what I am about to describe, you should include a list of your courses and information on any major projects you completed. If your GPA is at least 3.5, include it.

For everyone else, your education is important but it is not what is going to get you a job after your first job out of college. In fact, the college you attended will be irrelevant, except in one respect. Ivy League colleges are great places to build networks. And, as already stated, you should always network with your former classmates. But while being a Harvard MBA, for instance, may get you your first job, if you do not perform well at it, and the MBA from a community college did great in his first job after college, and if you are competing against each other for a job, he's getting the job offer, not you.

Under Education list the name of the school, the year you graduated, the degree you were awarded, and your Major. If you want, include your Minor. If you have an advanced degree, by all means include the title of your thesis or dissertation, as the case may be. And now the big question: Do you or do you not include the year you graduated?

Many people leave out the year because they are afraid of age discrimination. Ironically, the result is that when a recruiter or employer sees a résumé without the person's year of graduation, they immediately assume that the applicant is old. And, of course, if you get the interview, they will immediately know, pretty much, your age as soon as you walk in the door. So what are you hiding? And the question is not *when* you graduated but *what* you have done since you graduated. How have you used your education? It's your résumé; do what you feel is best for you. Not including the year of graduation is not a lie.

"Education" refers to accredited schools. Following Education should come, **Continuing Professional Education**. This section is important because, especially for "older" candidates, it shows employers that you have remained current in your field.

It does not matter if the course was at a school, an organization, or online. As noted earlier, it is what you learned that counts, not where you learned it. List the school/organization responsible for the class, the topic, the year, and a summary of what was covered in the course.

This brings us to the next section, **Certifications and Licenses**.

Obviously, list your certifications and licenses, the issuing authority, the date you received the certificate or license, and the expiration date, if any. Your studies toward the certificate or license, should not come under Continuing Professional Education, but rather be listed here, under Certifications and Licenses.

Next comes **Professional Memberships**. These are important because they show involvement in your industry. List them and the years in which you have been a member. Most importantly, include any roles you had/have within the organizations.

Remember how I said not to include a Professional Summary because no one cares what you think about yourself? Well, they do care what others think of you. And now is the time to brag:

Media Citations. List every time you have been quoted in an article. If you have half a dozen or so, include in the "Selected Accomplishments" section, "Recognized authority on ... (see 'Media Citations' below)." This shows that reporters and editors believe your opinions have merit. You should also include podcast, radio and television appearances. (Don't overdo it. If you have many, list the most recent and then add, "Full List Available Upon Request" at the top next to the "Media Citations" heading. Do the same for the next three sections as well.)

Speaking Engagements. List them. Note the organization which invited you, the topic and the date.

Publications. List the title of the article, the name of the publication, the number or date of the issue, page numbers, and any co-authors.

Awards & Honors. Include the awarding organization, the title of the award/honor, what it was for (if not self-evident), and the date it was presented.

Lastly we come to **Volunteer Activities.** As noted, with some companies, this is what could land you a job offer. Employers like to see that their employees are involved in the community. Everyone knows where they work and that makes them ambassadors. List the name of the organization, your titles, if you have any, your specific activities and their results. (Remember, if you have been unemployed for a long time, put your most recent volunteer activities under "Employment-Related Activities.")

I had one career counseling client who was unemployed for almost two years before she came to me. During that time, she volunteered for a local non-profit. She organized a fundraiser for them which brought in half a million dollars. She never thought of including it on her résumé because it was not "work." When she finally did include it, she not only started to get interviews and offers, but she transitioned from the for-profit to the non-profit sector. Volunteering is important!

One last thing: In addition to not having personal data, an Objective or a Professional Summary, do not end your résumé with "References Available on Request." It is a waste of space and makes you look like an idiot. What? You are not going to provide references if requested? Of course you will! Leave it out.

Now that you have your résumé, and the phone is ringing, it's time to get a job!

Part Three: Interviewing

Let's go over this again: The purpose of the cover letter is to get the recipient to look at the résumé. The purpose of the résumé is to get the interview. *If you are not getting interviews, you have a problem with your cover letter and/or résumé.* The purpose of the interview is to get the job offer. *If you are getting interviews but no offers, you have a problem with your interviewing skills.* Period. End of sentence. End of discussion.

One thing to always remember, just as it does not matter what you *write* in a cover letter but rather what the recipient *reads*, in an interview it does not matter what you *say*, what matters is what the interviewer(s) *hear.* I'll give you one example:

Years ago I had an interview and was asked about my weaknesses. First, I told them that I have trouble remembering people's names. I then said that to overcome it I "map" the room when I am in a meeting. Everyone nodded and commiserated. Then I said, "And I have no sense of direction."

Up until that moment I was hitting on all cylinders. The interview was going great. Then it got cold in the room. As I was answering the next question, I was trying to figure out what I had done wrong. Then I realized what had happened and I said the following:

"I want to return to my previous answer. When I said that 'I have no sense of direction,' I did not mean that I cannot follow instructions, or come up with a strategy and implement it, what I meant was that I am directionally challenged and can get lost going around a circle."

Everyone laughed and I got the job. Why? Because I knew what to do, how to prepare, how to act, how to follow-up and, perhaps most importantly, how to "read the room." I saw the body language of my interviewers. They stiffened up. They glanced at each other. They moved in their chairs, all signs that they were uncomfortable. Be cognizant of not only your own body language, but also that of your interviewers'.

Research

In real estate the saying is, "Location, location, location." With interviewing it is, "Research, research, research." You have to research the company, the interviewers and the employees.

One thing you cannot research is your competition. There will be three types: First, internal candidates. Their advantage is that they are known and know the company. You would have to learn the company way; they won't. On the other hand, they only know the company way; you can bring in new ideas. That's your advantage. Second, "friends of." They could be friends of board members, funders, employees. In other words, office politics. As with internal candidates, there is little you can do about them. Third, outside candidates just like you. Truth is, you can beat all three types, especially the latter. And I am now going to teach you how!

Here's a question you may not have considered: When do you start researching?

I once had a client who was a professional researcher. I pride myself on my research skills, but she put me to shame. When we met she showed me the one-page reports she had prepared on the companies to which she had applied – and a one-pager she had prepared on me! They took time to create, but they were excellent. And they were also a complete waste because none of those companies had invited her in for an interview. She had put the cart before the horse.

Not meaning to get ahead of myself, but when she finally landed interviews, and had one-page reports on the interviewers, she did not show them to them. When I asked her why, she told me that she was uncomfortable showing them because she did not want them to think that she was spying on, or stalking, them. I told her to always show her research, after all, she was applying to be a researcher! I also instructed her to explain that her reports began with the things about which she was confident, and ended with those items about which she had doubts. A week after we met, she had two interviews in the same day and two job offers the next day. Why? The interviewers saw the quality of her work.

In any event, you do not start researching companies in any great depth until you have an interview. It's simply a waste of your time, money and effort. You need to be focused on reality and the reality is that the majority of your applications will go unanswered. Her time would have been better spent networking and answering ads.

The first real contact with an employer will either be via email or phone. In the case of an email, all they will want is for you to give them some dates and times when you are available for a first (plan on two or more) interview. In the case of a call, it is not an interview; it is a call to set up the first interview. The only way you can blow the initial communication would be by not answering their questions or by being rude. So don't get flustered.

Hopefully, they will remind you for which job you applied. If they don't, and you created the Excel spreadsheet mentioned earlier, you are fine. But if they didn't, and you didn't, shame on you and shame on them. When it happens, just be honest. It happened to me once, a long time ago. I said, "I'm sorry. But I don't have my notes in front of me and I have applied for many positions. Can you please remind which job we are talking about?" There was no problem. She told me and we set up an appointment. It was not a big deal. It could have been if I had tried to manipulate her into telling me which job it was. She would have caught on and I would have looked like a fool. My advice always is to just be honest.

Now you have a real interview. So how do you research a company? First, study their website. Second, Google them to find articles or reports about their activities. Third, go to LinkedIn and look at their company page. Do the same on Facebook. Read their tweets and see who they are following on Twitter. And read their reviews on Yelp, Glassdoor.com, and similar sites (but, as I said previously, with a grain of salt).

Next you have to research the interviewers. People hire people they like, and they like people with whom they share something in common. Find out what that is, and use it. The company's website, LinkedIn and Google, should get you what you need.

For example, the interviewer asks you how you deal with difficult people. The normal response would be to use a client or customer as an example. But you know that the interviewer is on the board of his church, as are you. So you say, "Instead of telling you about a customer, let me give you an example that may resonate with you on a personal level. Like you, I am on the board of my church..."

At this stage you will, hopefully, be interrupted and the interviewer will want to know how you know about his board activities. And you simply tell him and add, "If I have the time, I always research the people with whom I meet so I can know how best to be effective." Perfect response. Now the interviewer knows that he or she can be confident about sending you to meet with whomever. You do your homework. You prepare.

What happens if you do not know with whom you are going to be meeting? First, ask. Tell the person arranging the interview that you want to thoroughly prepare, but don't make a federal case out of it. Perhaps they don't even know, which would be a red flag for you to ponder when deciding if you want to accept an offer, if they make one. The best you can do is to use LinkedIn. See who works in the department in which you presume you would be working. It's a guess, but it is the best you can do.

You have researched the company. You have researched the interviewers. Now you have to research the employees. How do you do that and why would you?

Well, if their bios are not on the company's website, you should be able to find their profiles on LinkedIn by searching for them by name or for the company and then clicking on the links to its employees. It is really that simple. The importance is that you want to get a feeling for the company. How long do people stay with them? Do they promote from within? And do you lack something that everyone else seems to have. For example, what if they all speak a foreign language and you don't. Don't worry about it. Because you have a good résumé, they already know. Yet, they are still interviewing you. So it probably does not matter. Just be aware of the differences, positive (you might have something that everyone else lacks!) and negative, so you will not be surprised. And, if the subject comes up, as always, the simplest, easiest, and best answer is just to tell the truth.

Before we get into the specifics of the different types of interviews, I want to digress for a moment and offer some advice to veterans:

Here are 10 things veterans should keep in mind when conducting a job search (and, fair warning, I will be repeating myself):

1. Civilians want to hire veterans but they are concerned. They can't directly ask questions about their concerns because they are afraid they will be sued or reported to the relevant authorities.

2. Their number one concern is the health of the veteran so raise the issue yourself. If you are healthy, tell them upfront. The 800-pound gorilla has left the room! If you have a visible disability explain what "reasonable accommodation" you need. If you have a hidden disability, explain what it is, what that means, and how you are controlling it. The key is that they

should understand that the disability is an irrelevancy. By raising the issue yourself, you are sending the message that (a) you know what they are worried about, (b) that you are honest and (c) you are direct - three things employers usually like in a candidate! Bottom line: As soon as *you* raise the issue, and explain it, then it is no longer an issue. The 800-pound gorilla is sitting in the corner of the room calmly eating a banana!

3. Civilians are ignorant about military life. When they ask about rank, don't answer with "E-4." They don't know what that means. They do know what a private, corporal, sergeant, lieutenant... are. Speak "civilian" not "military." The number one reason why veterans are not hired is a failure on their part to properly communicate with the civilian employer. Despite what some people will tell you, it is *not* the responsibility of the civilian employer to learn "military," it is *your* responsibility to learn "civilian."

4. If you are applying for a job similar or identical to what you did in the military (a truck driver, is a truck driver, is a truck driver; a warehouse manager, is a warehouse manager, is a warehouse manager), a civilian employer will understand you and you can talk about what you actually did.

5. If you are applying for a job totally divorced from what you did in the military, focus on the skills that made you successful. Never get into the details of what you did; it may scare them off. But, by all means, explain to them why your work was meaningful for you. It's a great way to respond to the "Tell us about yourself" opportunity which we will be discussing.

6. Civilian employers are prejudiced in favor of veterans because they believe veterans, with the possible exception of privates, are leaders, decision makers, do not need to be micromanaged, are team players, are honest, are reliable, understand the big picture, check their egos at the door, etc. Those are the traits on which you need to focus. When you interview make certain they know that you have been working

for X number of years in a culture where "No" is an unacceptable response and where there is no such thing as calling in sick! They will like that! Your new colleagues may not, but the boss will!

7. Civilian employers can be ignorant about military responsibilities. They think that "supervision" in the military is simply "barking" orders. They don't understand that even in a combat situation a commander (regardless of rank) needs buy-in from their troops. And, some are shocked to learn that some officers supervise more civilian than military personnel. If that was your situation, make sure it is understood. Explain what your responsibilities were. Proceed on the assumption that they will not know what you are talking about, even if it is something simple. What's obvious to you may not be obvious to them! For example, I had a full colonel rejected for a job because he did not have any "operational" experience. In fact, that was all he did but the word "operations" did not appear on his résumé. My client would not believe me... (Some say that that was just her way of not having to hire a veteran. I don't believe that because she engaged my services specifically to find high ranking veterans to fill the position.)

8. If you are applying for a non-profit job, focus on the fact that having volunteered for the military means that you put country above yourself and that you are a person who is interested in the greater good. Put differently, you are mission-focused; non-profits all have missions!

9. Don't confuse ignorance and stupidity. Not knowing what "E-4" means is one thing, not be willing to accept that a colonel knows about operations, is another. And then there was my favorite client. I called her and told her that I was submitting a West Point graduate. She was excited. She told all of her colleagues. Then she called me livid. "You said he had gone to West Point; it is not on his résumé!" I told her to hang on; maybe I sent the wrong résumé. Then I directed her attention to the last page, under

"Education," where it clearly said, "United States Military Academy." She said, "That's not West Point! It does not say West Point!" Ignorance or stupidity?

10. And, to end, one really crazy one: Never call a woman "Ma'am" unless you are applying for work in the former Confederacy. I have heard too many stories from (Yes, they admitted it to me!) and about women who rejected veterans because they were offended that they called them, "Ma'am." *That* is just plain stupid. (While some men don't like "Sir"ing, I have never heard of any man rejecting a veteran candidate because they referred to them as "Sir." That said, if they tell you to stop calling them "Sir," *stop!*)

Now it is time to consider the three types of interviews: Phone, video and in-person. We will consider each separately.

The Phone Interview

Remember when we were discussing communication and I pointed out that your body language and tone of voice are more important than your actual words? Well, on the phone you only have your tone of voice and words. Accordingly, it is crucial that you sound positive. Luckily, there is a simple way to ensure that your positive words are complemented by your tone.

It is an old salesman's trick. Have a mirror in front of you. That way you will remember to smile. You cannot sound negative if you are smiling. It is humanly impossible. So smile! But keep one thing in mind: You can sound sarcastic. Don't! And, also, don't smile if you are discussing something sad. You'll sound like an idiot!

If you are going to be at work during the call, best to sit in your car. Of course, if anyone sees you they will be suspicious, but better that they should see you than hear you, if you are in your office behind closed doors and someone just happens to be standing outside your door. You can always explain to the interviewer that you are at work. It happens all the time.

If you are home, get dressed. I don't mean to put on your business clothes, just don't be in your PJs. It is important that you feel professional so that you will sound professional. Again, have the mirror in front of you, and also your résumé. You will be nervous. You do not want to make any mistakes by misremembering something on your résumé. That could be fatal. And have pen and paper is not a bad idea. It is always good to take notes.

A phone interview is not in-depth. The idea is to screen you to make certain that the caller correctly understood your résumé, which presumably she reviewed prior to placing the call, and that you are, in fact, qualified for the position. Like the video interview, which we are about to discuss, from your perspective, its purpose is to get the in-person interview. So while you usually will not have a lot of time, you will have an opportunity to ask a few questions, at least you should. As a general rule, and this is especially true for the in-person interview, if an employer does not ask you if you have any questions, then that is a clear sign that they are inconsiderate and do not care about you, and more than likely, they don't care about their employees either. Any interview is a two-way street, and you have the right to ask questions. So why would you want to work for them if they do not afford you that courtesy?

If you don't have any questions, it is a clear sign that you are not really interested in the position. And saying, "You already answered all my questions," does not sound well at all. It is not a compliment. It sounds like you are "sucking up." You have to have questions, in addition to any clarifications you may have requested during the interview. Since time will be limited, I recommend asking these two:

"Who succeeds at your company? What type of person?" This goes to culture and management style and, surprisingly, some interviewers have a problem answering it. That already tells you something about them! What you want to know is if you will be a good fit. If they micromanage, and you can't stand being micromanaged, best to pass. In addition to serving the purpose of finding out about culture, although this does not always work, this question sends the message, the important message, that you don't want to waste your time or theirs. Employers should appreciate that.

The second question is, "What did the last person who held this position do that you would like to see continued, and what would you like to see done differently?" This question serves two purposes: First, it shows that you are a professional and not a gossip. Most people ask, "Why is this position available?" or "What happened to the last person who had this position?" It's none of your business. What do you care? How will the answer help you get the job or succeed in the job? It won't. What will is knowing what your predecessor did correctly and what needs to change.

74

Second, the question is a way of finding out if the position is new. And if it is new, you have a lot of questions to ask.

I can't tell you how many career counseling clients I have had who lost their most recent jobs because they were new positions and the company had not thought it through. It even happened to me years ago. You *have to* know if there is a budget for the position, including your compensation and benefits, as well as whatever you need to do the job. You also have to be certain that the person who is supervising you *wants* to supervise and was not just *told* to. And, getting back to budget, you have to make certain that the department paying you will be the one benefiting from your work. (That's what killed me. Luckily, the administrative assistant warned me what was coming and I was able to resign, having secured a new job, before my scheduled six-month review.) These are important questions. Don't be shy about asking them. They are totally legitimate. The only questions you should never ask are ones concerning proprietary information, work hours and vacation days. (More on that, later.)

So, you are dressed properly; you have your mirror and are smiling; you have your résumé in front of you; you have your questions to ask. Now what? As I said before, God gave us two ears and one mouth so we would remember to listen twice as much as we speak. If you are talking, you are not listening. If you are not listening, you are not learning. If you are not learning, you will not know what to say. Remember?

To digress, sort of, for a moment, never interrupt an interviewer. They hate it and it has cost some people jobs. It's rude. Don't do it!

Back to listening. Employers, interviewers, like to talk. Let them! They usually talk too much. They will tell you what they want to hear. Why? They are fed up with the hiring process. They want a body in the chair. They want you!

Another digression: You can learn everything you need to know about the company from their hiring process. If they are disorganized, slow, require input from too many people, it may not be the company for you.

In any event, they want to hire someone. So help them.

I once had a career counseling client who came to me for interviewing assistance. He told me that he had an interview for a business development role at a real estate company. His résumé was stellar. His cover letter was flawless. His interviewing was awful.

In response to my question, he told me that at his last interview the owner of the company had told him about their difficulties growing their *commercial* real estate division. They asked him to tell them about his experience growing sales. He told them all about his *residential* experience, which was exemplary and totally irrelevant and the reason he did not get the offer.

He obviously had *listened*, but he had not *heard*. Granted, his residential experience was better than his commercial, but they only cared about the latter, not the former. So I told him that next time he was in that situation, he should focus on his commercial experience which, frankly, would probably be better than the company's because, obviously, they would be having problems with their commercial business. Then, after talking about commercial, I told him to just add, "I have more significant residential experience and would be happy to tell you about it, if you want."

Next interview the same thing happened. This time he talked commercial and offered to tell them about his residential experience. They declined and offered him the job. LISTEN!

Finally, send the interviewer(s) a thank-you email. I'll teach you how when we discuss following-up after an interview. The same things goes for video, usually Skype, interviews, to which we now turn our attention.

The Video Interview

If you are applying for a job out of town, or if it is busy season and it is difficult for everyone to meet at the office, you may have a video interview. (In that case, the phone interview will probably be very short. The caller may just want to review your qualifications. This is usually done by a junior person who has no authority. But be nice, they can torpedo your candidacy!)

Video interviews are different from phone interviews in a number of ways. First, it is great evidence of whether or not you are comfortable with technology. Second, unlike with a phone, you can be seen, so body language, including eye contact, nodding, smiling and hand gestures, are now relevant. And third, you want to look professional. They know you are home, so be reasonable. For men, ladies you are on your own with this, putting on a tie and jacket is silly. You should wear a button-down shirt with a collar. By the way, looking professional, and this is also part of body language, includes not fidgeting, which is difficult. Woman twirl their hair; men stroke their beards (even if the don't have one!). We all do it. I read somewhere that we touch our faces two to five times a minute. Try not to do it in an interview, be it video or in-person. And one last difference, set the stage. What will the interviewers see? Make sure it is clean and, if there is something you can place behind you that will lead to a friendly conversation, do so.

I will use myself as an example. I am a vociferous reader. I bought a Kindle many years ago (I am on my third), because I literally ran out of shelf space. When I do a Skype interview, behind me are my books. I am almost always asked about them. And when we discover that we have read the same books, I always get the interview, whether it be for a job or, now, for acquiring new clients.

By the way, if you are taking the "call" at work, there is no problem sitting in your car. Try not to move the phone, as it is distracting. In the case of a video interview in a car, most employers will be understanding if it is not a perfect broadcast.

Other than these few points, everything else is the same as it was for the phone interview (minus the mirror, of course, because you will be able to see yourself on your computer and, hopefully, will remember to smile.) You need your résumé, but keep it below the camera so interviewer(s) will not realize you are looking at it. And you may have the opportunity to ask more than the two suggested questions. Shortly, we will discuss additional questions to ask.

The In-Person Interview

Congratulations! You did great. Your cover letter got them to look at your résumé. Your résumé got you the initial phone or video interview(s). Now you have been invited to partake of the Holy Grail: the in-person interview! Are you nervous? You better be. You have to appear confident, but fear is healthy. You don't want to assume the job is yours. You want to assume the job is yours *to lose,* otherwise, your show of confidence may turn into a display of pomposity.

Dress. If I have to tell you what appropriate dress is for a job interview, you have a serious problem. My advice is to always dress a little better than you would do on the job. If you don't know the dress code, clues may be found on the company's website or social media pages. In any event, always err on the side of conservative. Three simple rules to follow: Don't have any odor, don't accentuate you physical attributes (I can't put it more delicately than that!), and don't show off your wealth.

One last thing, for the ladies, and I am going to be blunt. Don't wear too much makeup and don't go for an interview looking like a supermodel. Unless you want the job of being the lure for men to visit the tradeshow booth or to come into the store so that someone else can sell to them, in other words, unless you want to be "eye candy," tone it down. Moreover, some bosses, bad bosses, don't like hiring attractive women because they think they will be a distraction, ironically, for both their male *and* female employees. It's stupid. It's wrong. It's real. Lead with your brains, not your body.

As for showing off your wealth, accessories will be noticed and you never know how people will react. Everything you wear sends a message. You want the interviewers to be focused on your expertise, not your style. There is a big difference between walking into an interview wearing a Rolex and walking in wearing a Timex. No one would even notice a Timex; they will notice a Rolex. What is the message you want to send? That you are wealthy?

Same for rings. As my LinkedIn readers know, a half dozen or so clients, who were great, all wore *very large* engagement rings. There was absolutely no logical reason why they were not getting job offers; they were getting plenty of interviews. They were knowledgeable, articulate, experienced, charming – everything an employer would want. But what was immediately noticeable were those rings. As soon as they removed them, they got job offers. Why? Who knows? Who cares?

Just to make sure there is no misunderstanding, if wearing your very large rings (I originally described them as "Hope Diamond-size"), are more important to you than getting job offers, wear them. Just remember, *it is your job search and you have to deal with the consequences.*

Many female writers, misrepresenting what I had written and ignoring the fact that my advice actually worked, was publicly confirmed by a number of readers, and "liked" by over 1,400, claimed I had advised to remove *all* engagement rings *and* wedding rings. Not so! And, unlike engagement rings which men do not wear, men do wear wedding rings, so this applies to everyone.

Being married is a legal status, so do not remove your wedding ring. And don't think that when they see the ring, interviewers will immediately assume you have children or plan to have children, and that it will be held against you. That is all nonsense. In fact, it could work in your favor! Parents cannot afford to jump from job to job. Employers like stability! (Which is why my advice pertained only to very large engagement rings, the ones that show opulent wealth.)

In any case, there is no longer a stigma attached to having children out of wedlock, so any female candidate could be(come) a mother, just as any male candidate could be(come) a father. So none of this matters. What does matter is that you make a great impression, not by flaunting your wealth, but by exhibiting your intelligence, experience, personality and maturity.

There is, of course, one exception to not showing off your wealth: If you are applying for a commission-based sales position, and you bought that Rolex or that Hope Diamond-size ring yourself, you can mention it as proof of just how good a salesperson you are. But, again, that could backfire. So I go back to my original advice, always err on the side of conservative.

For some professions, such as nursing, you have to know the proper dress code. To continue with the example, no, you should not show up for an interview wearing a nurse's uniform. But because nurses are not permitted to have long finger nails, or wear sharp or dangling jewelry, respect the code.

My favorite teaching assignment (Sorry, university students), was when I taught people in the trades: Plumbers, carpenters, electricians, and even a bricklayer. In one class, when we were discussing proper interview attire, I suggested that the guys show up in slacks, a shirt and tie. They vehemently objected to the tie. Nice trousers and shirt, that was fine, but a tie!?! After they were done telling me that they would look ridiculous, the youngest student, a plumber, raised his hand. He said that he had applied for a job and was one of around 10 applicants. He was the youngest and the least experienced. He got the job. On his first day he asked his boss why he chose him over the other candidates. "You were the only one wearing at tie," was the answer. I did not win many arguments with those students – probably why I liked them so much – but I won that one.

Your appearance has to be professional. Wherever you work, whatever your role, you are a professional. None of this "white collar – blue collar" nonsense! Of course standards are different. For example, obviously, working at a plumbing company is different than working at an accounting firm. Let's focus on those places that have high standards where appearance counts.

If you want to work at such a company, and you decided to have every visible square centimeter of your skin tattooed and anything on your body that could be pierced, pierced, that's on you. There are dress codes. Some businesses do not permit visible tattoos or visible piercings, above a set number. If you have them, lose them or cover them up. It's not discrimination (unless the tattoos or piercing are for religious reasons). Discrimination, illegal discrimination, is against people of a certain class such as religion, gender, nationality, medical condition and the like. You may be "crazy" to have done this to your body, but that kind of "crazy" is not protected. You made a choice and now you have to live with the consequences.

Punctuality. Except in the case of bad weather, never arrive more than 15 minutes early for an interview. It will be interpreted as a sign that you have problems with time management. In an interview, *everything* counts. The interview does not begin when you sit down to talk; it begins when you enter the building (for that matter, the parking lot). Always arrive on site early. Give yourself ample time in case something happens en route. Why? Because, there is no excuse for being late, and if you are late, you may not get the interview and, even if you do, it is unlikely you will get an offer.

Yes, there are always exceptions. And that is why you have to request a phone number to call in case of emergency. If your appointment was at Noon, and you left your home at 11:00 AM for what would normally have been a 45-minute trip, and there was an accident along the way, and you called, you will be out of luck. If you left at 10:00 AM, based on the experience of my career counseling clients and candidates for my executive recruiting clients, you'll get a second chance. There is a big difference between calling at 10:30 to say there was an accident and you *may* be late, and calling at 11:30 and saying you *will* be late.

Electronics. I cannot tell you how many times employers have called me, after interviewing a candidate, to complain that the individual's pocket and bag were buzzing, humming, beeping and ringing and the candidate kept apologizing but was unable to turn the devices off, or even, in a few cases, find them in their bags. Turn OFF all of your electronics. Take notes with pen and paper. If you have to have your phone on, apologize and explain why. And the reason better be on par with the person I interviewed whose wife was due to give birth any day.

Just a reminder, in addition to bringing pen and paper, bring some copies of your résumé. It is amazing how many interviewers cannot find candidates' résumés! Also, have samples of your work with you. Don't bring them out unless asked.

Receptionist. Be nice to the receptionist. She is important. If she reports back – and yes, the smart employers always ask the receptionist about the candidate's behavior – that you were a jerk, you are not getting a job offer. How can you make certain she likes you? Simple; shake hands with her. All day long she sees professionals greeting each other. They always shake hands. She, rightly, considers herself a professional. Offer your hand. Be polite. And when she informs the person with whom you are meeting that you arrived, thank her and leave her alone.

Here is a question that I am sometimes asked: What do you do if you are kept waiting more than 15 minutes? Well, I can only tell you what I have done. After 15 minutes I asked the receptionist what was happening. She said she did not know. After 20 minutes I thanked her and started to leave. At that point the man I was supposed to meet with came out. He stopped me. I told him that as far as I was concerned, one of the rudest things a person can do is to keep someone else waiting. It shows a complete lack of respect for their time. I then said that if I had been informed that there was an emergency, it would have been different. But, I told him, no one communicated with me at all. This was just rudeness or incompetence and, if this was how a candidate was treated, I did not want to know how they treated their employees. I was perfectly calm. I did not raise my voice or appear agitated. As I was leaving the building, the receptionist, with whom I had shaken hands – you see, I actually do know what I am talking about – came running after me. She had heard me. She told me that that person keeps people waiting all the time and no one likes him and she was thrilled that I had put him in his place. A week later, the owner called me to apologize. (No, I did not ask why it took him a week!) He informed that the man had been fired and he invited me in for an interview. I thanked him and declined as I had already accepted another position.

And that reminds me of something else: *Never stop your job search until you have an offer in-hand.* Things happen. It isn't real until it's real. Wait, as the expression goes, until the fat lady to sings!

Which brings me to another question I get: What happens when you accept a job and, before you start, or after you have started, you get a call about your dream job? Never accept it. It will harm your reputation. You made a commitment; honor it. And even if it is more money, how do you know you will be happy there? It is not worth the risk.

Greeting. After a few minutes, the person with whom you are to meet comes out, offers her hand, and introduces herself. You rise, you look her straight in the eyes, smile, give her a firm handshake and say, "Thank you for inviting me to interview. I really appreciate it." If you don't say "thank you" at the beginning and end of every interview, the odds are you will not get an offer.

As I mentioned earlier, a firm handshake is critical. It shows confidence. Everything you do, your body language, must exude confidence. Sit up straight; stand up straight; walk with conviction; look people in the eye; speak clearly; lean forward when something interests you; sit back to contemplate; gesture with your hands; exhibit confidence and friendliness. That is what you do - even more so if you are "old."

Let's discuss eye contact.

As we all know, when we are speaking with someone, and they break eye contact, we suspect something is not right. They are distracted; they might be bored. But when you are being interviewed, boredom is not the problem, at least it should not be.

There actually is a science to this. When you look up (think of every test you ever had in school), you are trying to remember. No problem looking up. Looking down is a problem. If you look down and to your right, that means you are trying to construct an honest answer that will be understood. But, if you look down and to your left, think of your heart, that means you are becoming emotional and are about to lie.

Two problems with this: First, as far as the significance of eye movement goes, most people don't know right from left, so don't look down. Second, good liars know all this and they never break eye contact. Nevertheless, there is a way to spot "good" liars, but I have to keep some secrets to myself; I can't reveal everything!

Bottom line: Don't break eye contact. When you speak to someone, look at them.

No negativity. Never, ever, say anything negative about a current or former employer or colleague. NEVER! So what do you say when they ask you why you are looking for a new job? You tell the truth. You don't say, "I am working for a bunch of idiots." You say, "I have had a good run, but it is time to move on. I am looking for professional advancement and growth." This is the ideal opportunity for you to ask the interviewers about their company's policies in regard to training and professional development. And don't worry; most interviewers have heard it all before. As with everything else, it's not a big deal unless you make it a big deal. Sell it with your tone of voice.

You will likely be asked about your weaknesses. (We'll deal with this question again later.) By definition, this is a negative. You have to tell them at least one weakness. We are all human. We all have them. Saying you can't think of one, or that you don't have any, makes you look foolish. And if you are telling the truth, it means you are not self-aware. No one wants an employee who is not self-aware. So tell them the negative and end on a positive. It's the same for any negative:

Why is there a three-year gap on your résumé?

I robbed the Bank of England but, ironically, that makes me a better employee because I learned...

I know it's silly, but it is something you will remember. Tell the truth. Don't make any excuses. Take responsibility for your actions. It's called "being an adult." And then say something positive about the experience. Believe me, I have gotten jobs for people who have been fired and who had been in jail. They followed my model and they found employment.

Honesty. I hope you are offended by this but it is incumbent upon me to reiterate what I have already written: If you lie on your résumé or in an interview, you may be fired for cause. Don't lie. Don't embellish. Don't spin. Just tell the truth. Keep it short. Keep it simple. When someone explains a difficult situation succinctly, they usually stay out of trouble. However, those who talked too much, just dig themselves in deeper and deeper.

Listen. Again, if you are talking, you are not listening. If you are not listening, you are not learning. If you are not learning, you won't know what to say. Listen! Take notes! As you will find out in a few minutes, notes are important. You have to remember some things you are told and some things you are asked. And in the name of all that is holy, NEVER INTERRUPT AN INTERVIEWER!

I vs. We. Many people are shy. They don't like to brag. They do not like talking about themselves. When you brag, you sound pompous and no one hires pompous people. So how do you brag without sounding like a braggart?

The first time you are asked about something you have done, begin with something like this: "I am happy to tell you, but first I want to make something clear. I have been fortunate to work with some very good people. But for now, I am going to focus on work I did on my own or on my contribution to the team effort. I just want you to know that I know that there is a 'we' behind the 'I.' " Now you can brag all you want!

One thing you should avoid is humor. Don't tell jokes. They will backfire. Someone will be offended. No jokes. No politics, religion or sex. There is no place for any of it and it will only get you into trouble. The only exception is self-deprecating humor, when you make fun of yourself. But even then, be careful.

Succinct and direct. Too often employers have called me after interviewing a candidate and told me, "You sent us the type of person we wanted. Great on paper. But he was nervous and wouldn't stop talking. We could not get a word in edgewise." When you are asked a question, answer that specific question. Don't give a history lesson. You can always ask, after you have given the short version, if they would like to hear more about this, that, or the other thing. If they want to, great; if not, no problem.

Ask questions. We will get to questions momentarily, but the important point right now is that, and I know I am repeating myself, if you don't have questions to ask, that means you are not really interested in the job.

Ask for the job. At the end of the interview, ask for the job. This does not mean, "May I please have the job?" What it means is, you have to show interest and enthusiasm. Too often employers have told me that the candidates they have interviewed (not mine!) just did not seem all that interested in the job. Show interest and enthusiasm. Tell them you are more interested now than when you arrived. As I said earlier, thank them again for interviewing you. Then ask about follow up. For reasons that will become clear, this will be very important. If they tell you they will be in touch without a timeline, so be it. If they say they will be in touch, or you should get back to them in a couple of weeks, great! Thank them and leave. We'll discuss later what to do when you do not hear from them.

For now, let's get to the heart of the interview, asking and answering questions.

Questions to ask. I believe that the questions you ask are more important than the answers you give to the interviewers' questions, which is why "Question to ask" comes first. I am not talking about the questions you will ask when you need clarification on something you are being told. These are your questions, independent of what you have been told:

- *Why did you want to interview me?* This is a great question with which to begin if they did not already tell you. Why? Because, as your first question, beginning your part of the interview where you are asking the questions, it forces the interviewer(s) to be positive. Moreover, if you know that they like A, B and C, you will then know that it is important for them to also be aware of D and E. Briefly tell them.

- *How did you prepare for this interview? What do you know about me?* This is an important question to ask if you are "known." Did they read your articles? Did they watch your videos? Did they listen to your podcasts? Did they read the articles in which you were quoted? If not, then you need to make certain they really know the real you, otherwise, it may not work out. You may not be a fit.

- *Why are you following X on Twitter?* If you don't have a Twitter account, open one. As noted earlier, you can use it to promote your LinkedIn articles. But it is also good for researching. Look at their Twitter account and find someone or a company that is unique and ask why they are following them. "Why are you following the British embassy? Are you planning to expand into Europe?" They probably will not know the answer. That's alright. The question served its purpose. You told them just how good you are at preparing for meetings. And when they ask the boss about the "follow," she probably won't know either but, in all likelihood, she'll want to meet the person who asked the question.

- *Press.* I had a job that did not last long. To put it mildly, we were not a fit. Hindsight is, of course, 20/20 and one warning sign was when I confessed that I could not find any press coverage about them and asked why. The director said there wasn't any. He explained that it was too complicated because everything would have to be approved by the funder. As I found out later, there was probably a very good reason why the funder did not want any publicity. But this is rare.

Ask questions about press releases they have issued or stories written about them. "I saw in the *Herald* that a couple of years ago you announced you were going to do X. What happened with that? It sounds interesting. If I get the job, will I be involved with it?" Again, they may not even know what you are talking about, but that's fine. You got your message across: You prepare well for meetings.

- *I saw in the LinkedIn Profile of X – I believe he was the last person who had the job – that he was responsible for A, B, C and D. The job description you shared with me does not include D, but does include E and F. Why?* If you can, find the Profile of the last person who had the job for which you are being considered, compare what they wrote about their responsibilities with the job description. Ask about any differences. And if there are none, ask why because that could be a sign that there is no growth in the position. Regardless, this is a question the interviewers should be able to answer and, again, it shows your research skills.

- *What would you like to see continued that the last person who had the position did, and what would you like to see done differently?* If you did not already ask the current interviewers (they may be different from the ones you spoke to over the phone or by video), ask this question and remember to explore in-depth if it turns out that it is a newly created position.

- *If I were to get the job, how would I be able to make your life easier?* This may be the most important question you ask. You can use the answer in the thank-you email you will send. I'll explain why when we get to the all important matter of follow-up. For now, just remember to write down the answer!

- *Who succeeds here?* Even if you asked the interviewers earlier, remind them and say you would like to discuss their answer further. It is important to delve deeper into the issue of fit. When I asked the question, at the job that did not work out, I got a rather bland answer. I frankly do not even remember what it was. And I am not saying that they were trying to deceive me. I honestly believe that it never donned on them to tell me that they were extreme liberals who believe that Political Correctness should be the law of the land. As readers of my LinkedIn articles know, I was fired, first and foremost, for having mentioned God when talking to a group of students about networking, because it could have been offensive to atheists! (Remember, two ears, one mouth?) Luckily, my boss was kind enough to put it in writing so there is no question about the accuracy of what you just read. You may not be so lucky as to have a boss so inclined to put, figuratively speaking because "fingers to keyboard" just doesn't sound good, pen to paper. Learn from my mistake. Dig!

Not a digression, but an aside. I was talking to my boss about the development of apps. I mentioned to him that I had read in a column in *Inc.* magazine that one developer found that fewer options were better. I also said that, if I remembered correctly, in Walter Isaacson's biography of Steve Jobs, he wrote that Jobs had come to the same conclusion. I then asked him what he reads. He told me he did not have time to read. That's when I knew I probably had made a mistake. So now I would ask interviewers, *What do you read?* If something is important to you, and it is part of who you are, make certain you share it to some degree with whomever will be your direct supervisor and perhaps also, your future colleagues.

- *Is there anything you feel I should clarify?* This is a tough one and I honestly don't know what to advise. I include it because one career counseling client told me, passionately, that he always asked at the end of an interview, "Is there anything problematic that you would like to ask me?" I did not like that because, as the final question, the interview would end on a negative. So I tweaked it to make it neutral. But I am still not certain if it is a good idea. I have never asked it, his way or mine. It's your interview. You decide. It might be helpful which is why I have included it.

A reminder: Never ask about working hours or vacations until you have been offered the job. It always comes across as your first priority not being work. That is not the message you want to send! Neither is admitting that your dream is to start your own business! They'll hear, "Train me to be your competitor!"

Of course, before you get a chance to ask questions you will have to answer some.

Questions to answer. One day a man called me. He had not had to look for a job in 25 years. A year earlier, his daughter had graduated from college. She had purchased a number of books on interviewing. He borrowed them and made a list of all the questions the authors had advised that interviewers "always" asked. He had a list of well over 50 questions. He also had had two interviews and in neither were any of the questions the so-called "experts" said he would be asked, asked! I assured him that if he came to me for my interview services I would give him a half dozen more questions that he could be certain he would not be asked. He laughed, signed up, and did very well in his subsequent interviews.

The only questions you are guaranteed you will be asked in an interview relate to the job description. That is what I focus on when I conduct a mock interview. But I also ask the following because, even if you only have one interview, you really are having two.

There are two types of interviews: Technical and behavioral, sometimes referred to as hard-skills and soft-skills. The former tests your knowledge (the focus of the job description); the latter checks your personality. Given the choice, admittedly an exaggeration – although you might be surprised – between a candidate with exemplary skills but a lousy personality, and a candidate with good skills and a great personality, it is the latter who will receive the offer. Remember, people only hire people they like.

One word of warning: Never say "transferrable skills." When you say that, in response to the question, "Have you done this before?" and you haven't, the employer will hear, "Listen. I have not done this but, do me a favor and consider me anyway." Employers do not have to do you any favors. If you have not done the work, instead of saying "No, but I have transferrable skills," say, "No, but I have transferrable *accomplishments*," and then tell them what they are!

Here are the questions I believe you may be asked:

- *How did you prepare for this interview?* I'll be honest; no one is ever going to ask this question. But it is a great question and it *should* be asked. So if you are interviewed by an employer who has read this book, be prepared to answer it. Again, just tell the truth. They want to learn how you prepare for meetings.

Very often there is an ulterior motive behind questions. As I mentioned early when discussing the importance of being well-read, if you are asked a question out of left field, think about it for a few seconds. Ask yourself why you are being asked the question. But don't get paranoid; sometimes a question is just a question.

- *If we hire you, where will our company be in five years?* This is a chance to learn how the candidate thinks. Of course, it is also somewhat of a trick question, as the candidate can't possibly know and, unless they are being considered for the CEO position, they should not be focused on the company but on the specific role they hope to obtain. Moreover, it would be presumptuous to tell an owner what they, a candidate, are going to do with *their* company. This is how I would respond:

I would not be so presumptuous as to tell you where you will be in five years. There are too many variables I would need to know to make any prediction. In any case, almost all countries that operated on five-year plans are no longer in existence. What I can tell you is that during any five-year span of my career, I have always moved forward. I don't plan to stop now. My definition of failure is if the person taking over from someone gets the same job description the current employee received when they were hired. That means there was stagnation. My job descriptions have always changed. I have never stagnated.

I believe they will like that answer.

- *What do you know about us?* Obviously, tell them but it is not enough just to regurgitate their website. Show them that you thought about it. Say something like: "I know you provide services A, B and C. I would be interested in knowing why you don't offer D and E as well. It would seem like a logical progression." And, of course, mention what you discovered on their social media and when you Googled them.

- *Why do you want to work here?* This is your chance to shine and to differentiate yourself from your competition. They will use this as an opportunity to lavish praise on the company. No one falls for it. What you will do is give logical reasons that will show that you did your homework and that will also put them at ease about your candidacy. If it is true, say something like this: "I saw the LinkedIn Profiles of your employees. They have been with you for a good number of years and you promote from within. That is what I am looking for." This is especially good for "older" candidates because the fear is that they will not stay long on the job. This answer should help to dispel that concern.

Another answer which, again, shows your research skills, could be: "I saw in the press that your leadership has received community service awards and that you are active in the community. I want to work for a company that is community-minded." This shows that you buy in to their mission and culture.

Which reminds me; if the company has a mission statement, memorize it. Mention it. If you don't, I can almost guarantee you that you will not get an offer.

- *What are your weaknesses? What was your greatest failure?* This is another example of a question with an ulterior motive. As I said earlier, they want to know that you are self-aware. Tell them. And tell them how you overcame the weakness, or what you learned from the failure. We have all had them. Don't be ashamed, in fact, be proud! Truth is, they are really asking, "Why *shouldn't* we hire you?"

- *What are your strengths? What was your greatest success?* Obviously, this is the opposite side of the same coin. Don't just tell them the "what," but also the "how" and, most importantly, the "why." For "older" candidates, another concern, in addition to worrying that you will not stay long on the job, is that you are not open to change. That should be the emphasis of your answer. Give them a couple of examples where you initiated or implemented change. (Later, when we focus on discrimination, I will delve deeper into how "older" candidates should interview.) The question they are really asking is, "Why *should* we hire you?"

- *What are you most proud of? Why did you do something a certain way?* Tell them. The question really is, "How do you deal with criticism?" Regardless of your answer, even if your way is there way, a smart interviewer will criticize you. Don't take the bait. Consider what they say, thank them, and tell them why you had not considered it. If you don't think it is a good idea, by all means, tell them. That's alright. Just explain your logic. And if you think it would have been a good idea, tell them why. Just don't become defensive. You must show them that you take criticism well and are willing to change – especially if you are a Millennial or, as just noted, an "older" candidate. (Ironic, isn't it?)

- *When did you have to overcome adversity?* This is a great question, especially for "older" candidates, as we will discuss within the context of coping with discrimination. But it is also a good place to talk about how you have overcome a disability or disorder from which you "suffer." This can also be the focus of the "Tell us about yourself opportunity" which we will get to momentarily. For now, suffice it to say, that I have worked, in this regard, with autistic, dyslexic, and homosexual persons, as well as those dealing with Attention Deficit Disorder and Post Traumatic Stress. You can turn a negative into a positive. (And before anyone complains, they "suffer" and are "negatives" not because I say so but because those were the word my clients used!)

- *Why are you looking to leave your current job? Why did you leave your previous jobs?* This one is almost always asked. (It they don't ask it in the interview, it will probably be on the application form.) Just tell the truth. Keep your answers short. Don't bad mouth. If you don't make a big deal out of it, they won't. But please, don't do what most people do. Don't give a history lesson about the company and gush over how great a place it was to work. The interviewer does not care. Literally, a few nice words followed by the reason, will suffice.

By the way, and I have heard this from enough attorneys to believe I am correct, if you lost your job, and were paid Unemployment, you can honestly say you were not fired. You were laid off.

- *Tell us about yourself.* This is another question which you are likely to be asked and a great chance to, once again, differentiate yourself.

Did you catch my error? I said that "this is another *question*." It is not. It is an *opportunity* of which most people do not take advantage. They foolishly summarize their résumés. Well the interviewer(s) already read the résumé. That's why you are being interviewed. So what should you do?

Tell them something about yourself, as a professional, that is not on your résumé and will let them see what type of a person you truly are. I'll give you three examples because this is the opportunity with which most people have the most difficulty. All of these examples are true. The last is mine:

> *I was on the police force for only two months when I had to deliver my first baby. A year later I delivered my second, and thankfully last. About five years later, I single-handedly captured two armed bank robbers and recovered the money. I was more scared delivering the babies than going after the robbers!*

And when the officer told me that story, it was very funny. I cannot do it justice. But it told me a great deal about him as a person, not just as a professional, and I had no hesitancy whatsoever submitting him to my client.

*One of my responsibilities was providing
security at construction sites. One of the buildings
that was being built was a school for girls. It was
boring. Guard duty is boring until it isn't any more.
But when the construction was over, and I saw the
expression on the faces of the girls who were going
to school for the first time in their lives, it was all
worthwhile.*

Obviously, this story was told to me by a veteran who had served in Afghanistan. I tell it here because it took a good hour and a half to come up with it. He kept telling me he was "only a soldier," and did not have any experience like the one I had which I am about to share. But we found one. And you can too.

Now for my story. I have told it many times. It has been dubbed, "The Big Bird Story."

If you have done your research, you should know what will resonate with the interviewer(s). When I have been given the "Tell us about yourself" opportunity, I always changed it slightly and responded, "I'm going to tell you about my best day on any job." My goal was to let them know what is not on my résumé. I wanted them to know about me as a person. So I would tell them this story and, so far, it has never failed (well once when my competition was an internal candidate) because it's true and it resonates, especially with non-profits. Plus it's unexpected because it has absolutely nothing whatsoever to do with my accomplishments, or my actual work responsibilities, which is what they expect to hear. And, it has a surprise ending:

*This was my best day on any job:
Years ago, I was the assistant director of a
Jewish Federation in New Jersey. We had a YM-
YWHA. The program directors had an idea. They
wanted to have a community fair for Hanukah. It
would not be a fundraiser (my responsibility) but
simply a "thank-you" event. A fun day where we
would sell tickets for games, sell some food, and if
we broke even we would be happy. If we made a few
bucks, great; if we lost a few, who cares?
At the meeting we had to discuss their idea, the
directors, all young women, looked at me and said*

that they needed a volunteer to dress up as a cartoon character. I realized I had no choice in the matter, saw no point in arguing, and, frankly, I wanted to do it. So I agreed.

I did, however, have one condition. I told them, "It has to be a manly character." They chose Barney! That's Barney the dinosaur, not Barney Rubble.

If you need to lose eight pounds in four hours, I know how to do it! The costume was huge. There was so much foam rubber I could barely fit through my office door – sideways!

We thought it was a great idea. At the time Barney was very popular. All the kids had little Barneys at home. So when I walked in to the gymnasium where the Fair was being held, we all expected the children to go nuts. And they did...but not the way we expected.

The smaller children were scared stiff and went running to their mothers. (The older kids just pulled my tail!) The little ones, who we were doing this for, wanted nothing to do with me. I was a seven-foot tall monster, not the Barney they knew and loved.

It was a failure. But it was only a failure in choice – we chose the wrong character, not concept. The following year we did it again only this time I was Big Bird.

Big Bird, by definition, is supposed to be big. It's in his name! This time, when I entered the gym, the kids went nuts the right way. They were beside themselves with excitement. Especially one little girl, who ran up to me, grabbed my leg, and hugged with all her might. After a few minutes I had to pry her off because she was cutting off the flow of blood! So we held hands. For four hours we held hands. When I had to take a break her father would take her from me. When I returned, she would be waiting by the door and we would go walking around hand-in-hand or with her hugging my leg.

At the end of the Fair I whispered to her father that I wanted to give her a hug. I explained that I could not bend over to pick her up because the costume head would fall off and I might hurt her because I had no peripheral vision. So he picked her up and she gave me a hug.

There are three hugs children give: There's the "nice to see you/welcome home, now I'm going back to play my video game" hug. There's the "thank you for the birthday present now I'm going to go play with it" hug. And then there's the nightmare hug. That's the hug where they are scared and hold on for dear life because they know you will protect them. That's the hug I got!

Don't get me wrong; she was not scared. I was not protecting her from anyone. She simply loved Big Bird and gave me the passionate hug. Then I had to signal to her father to pull her off of me.

When he put her on the floor, she took a couple of steps back. This was the first time that I actually had a good look at her. She was about six- or seven-years old. I waved at her; she waved at me and said, "Bye-bye Big Bird." I waved to everyone and went to my office.

I got out of the costume. I looked like something the cat dragged in. My clothes were all wrinkled and I was covered in perspiration. With a bottle of water in my hand, and a towel over my shoulder, I went into the lobby and noticed the little girl's mother. I went over to her and said, "I have to tell you, no one has ever hugged me the way your daughter did."

She looked at me like I was the biggest pervert on the planet. I had assumed she knew who I was. I immediately introduced myself:

"I'm Bruce Hurwitz. I'm the Federation's assistant director. I was Big Bird."

Her expression immediately changed. She got all misty-eyed, looked at me and said,

"Bruce, my daughter has autistic tendencies. When she said 'Bye-bye Big Bird' to you it was the first time she ever spoke to anyone outside of the immediate family or her teacher." And then she thanked me.

Interviewing

And that was my best day at ANY job!

Two things I want to point out: First, I said the directors were "young women." That is to send a message that I have experience working with different age groups. Second, and more importantly, I said that the directors chose the character but, when I said it was a failure, I said "we chose the wrong character." If they pick up on it is to send the message that I am a team player.

This version is a little long. The officer's story, and the veteran's, are closer to the proper length. But when I have the time, I give the full version. The result is always that three-quarters of the women, and half the men, are in tears. If I don't think it will be appreciated, I use something similar – and shorter!

Before continuing with the interview process, I want to talk about questions you should not answer:

There are legal questions. Those are easy. Any question which directly relates to the job is legal. But, there are illegal questions. And there are crooks. Let's deal with these in reverse order.

Crooks. The only time an employer needs to know a candidate's Social Security Number is if they are going to do a background check on the candidate. The only reason to do a background check is as a condition of employment. The process is simple. The employer makes you a conditional offer of employment, dependent upon the results of the background check. (This should be after they have checked references.) At that point, if you want the job, you give them your Social Security Number on an authorization form. (Just for the record, they have to share the results with you and give you time to respond and correct any errors.) That's for an *employer*.

As for *recruiters*, there is NEVER a reason to give a recruiter your Social Security Number unless the recruiter, representing the employer, is making the conditional offer of employment. Then you want the conditional offer of employment in writing, and a form authorizing the background check, clearly stating its purpose and that you will be informed of the results prior to any final determination being made so, and this has happened, any incorrect information can be addressed.

When filling out the form authorizing the background check, you will need to provide your full name and date of birth. Until then, neither the recruiter, nor the employer, needs to know your

SSN or where or when you were born. You don't know these people, but you should know about identity theft.

And one more thing – NEVER pay anyone to get you a job. NEVER! Career counselors promise to *help* you get a job, not to *get* you one. Recruiters are paid by the employers, never the candidates. And there is no such thing as an "application fee." Period. End of sentence. End of discussion.

This brings me to our next subject, illegal questions:

Illegal Questions. Any question dealing with a protected status is illegal. So, going back to your date of birth, you cannot be asked your age. You can be asked, for example on a job application form, when you graduated from college. Well, isn't that revealing your age? You probably graduated when you were 22, so do the math.

But that's not necessarily so. Some people finish a four-year degree in three and some finish in five. And some (literally) graduate with one of their grandchildren. So the date of graduation does not mean much.

"Where were you born?" is an illegal question. The only legal question an employer or recruiter can ask in this regard is, "Are you authorized to work in the United States?" That's it. But if you have a Spanish sounding name, received your undergraduate and graduate degrees from the University of Madrid, and note on your résumé that you are fluent in Spanish, the assumption is going to be that you were born in Spain.

Who cares? The employer might. And it could be a good thing. Odds are, if the person is a bigot and does not like the Spanish, you would not have gotten an interview. Being of Spanish birth may mean that you have a Spanish, or rather EU, passport, which may appeal to the employer if she does business in the EU. So if a job responsibility is to travel to the EU, asking if that is a problem is perfectly legal. And if you reply that you have an EU passport, so much the better. That could be the difference between you getting the job or someone else.

"Do you have a disability?" Illegal. The only question you can be asked is, "Is there any reason why you cannot fulfill the requirements of the position?" If there is, you have to tell the employer and if you need a "reasonable accommodation," the employer must provide it. But don't assume that what you consider "reasonable" is something she would consider "reasonable."

"What is your religion?" Illegal except if it is relevant to the job. For example, a non-profit created to support persons of a particular faith can restrict the CEO position to a person of that faith. Or, if your religion prohibits you from, let's say, working on the Sabbath, you have to tell the employer. We will deal with this, and health issues, later.

And there are more. "Are you married?" "How long?" "What does your spouse do?" "Where are your relatives from?" "Do you have children?" "How old are they?" "Are you planning on having children?" "What clubs or associations do you belong to?" The list never ends. The question is, What do you do when asked an illegal question?

Why would anyone ask an illegal question?

First, they are ignorant. They don't know the law.

Second, you are having a friendly conversation. They hire people they like. They want to like you. The only way they can like you is to get to know you, so they ask you about your family. In other words, they are naïve (I originally wrote "stupid," but that may be too harsh).

Why would you want to work for someone like that? How long are they going to stay in business? Eventually they'll be sued and they'll lose.

But, still, you need the job, so what are your options?

First, answer the question. If you don't care, why not?

Second, if you are comfortable, answer the question but immediately tell the interviewer that it is illegal and they could get into trouble. Then, tell them how to legally find out what they want to know, if it's possible. This may be appreciated and a bit feared because they may think you are threatening a law suit. (This is what I have done in the past and, no, I have never sued.)

Third, tell the interviewer that the question is illegal and you are uncomfortable answering it. This may be respected and, again, a bit feared. And it could end your candidacy.

Remember, the interview process is a two-way street. You will learn a great deal about the corporate culture and decision making from how the interview in conducted. Is an employer who lacks basic HR knowledge really the person for whom you want to work?

Lastly, what should you do if an employer gives you an assignment, either before the in-person interview (a condition, if you will, for getting it) or after the interview?

Some employers, with the knowing assistance of in-house recruiters, and (I hope) less frequently outside recruiters (of which I am one), go through a hiring process not to fill a position but to get free advice about how to overcome a problem they are facing. Here is what happens:

XYZ Company is losing market share. The new competitors are appealing to cohorts with which XYZ has no experience. They decide to create a new position, Outreach Business Developer, with the purpose of reaching out to those cohorts. They advertise and announce a good salary. The résumés come in and the interviews begin.

Once they have confirmed that the candidate is qualified, they go through the motions and then say, "If you are still interested in the position, we would like to receive from you a plan outling what you would do during your first six-months on the job. Who would you approach? How would you approach them? And why would you choose them?"

This can be perfectly legitimate. I have had executive recruiting clients (employers) do it. They always hired someone. At first, after receiving the request, my candidates would call and ask me if the job was real, because they had seen this before. That is why today, learning from the experience, I ask my clients what they will request of candidates and then I make certain they know that the request will be made. There are no surprises.

But how should you respond to the request?

Tell them that you will be happy to provide a one- or two-page outline of how you have done similar things in the past. Gauge their response.

Then, say that you will be happy to provide names of a few companies that you would reach out to, but, for obvious reasons, you would not be comfortable providing names and contact information.

If they are legit, they will respect you. If they are not legit, they will ask, "What do you mean by 'for obvious reasons'?" Your response should be, "Confidentiality."

Again, if they are honest, they will respect you. If they are not...

Finally, a question that sometimes comes up is, "How do I deal with my health issues." It is important, so let's consider it:

A few years ago I was invited to participate in a panel discussion on interviewing which was focused on veterans and the disabled. (And, no, I was not crazy about the juxtaposition but I understood the intent of the organizers and let it go.) One of the attendees, I believe he was a veteran, asked the question, "When should I tell an employer about my disability?"

The panel moderator asked one of the other panelists to respond. She said, "As long as it has nothing to do with your ability to do the job, say nothing."

This is not an uncommon response. Last year I spoke to a group of students. The same question was asked. Before I had a chance to respond, their teacher said, "After they offer you the job."

Terrible advice! Worse than the response of my former fellow panelist.

What's the problem?

You have a disability. It has nothing to do with your ability to do the job, so you don't tell the employer. That may be fine. But what if the employer looks at it differently? What if the employer is thinking safety? They are located on the 20th floor of a 30-story building. What if there is a fire? You'll still get the job only now the employer will know to report the issue to the building's Safety/Security Director before there is a crisis. But there is now the little matter of the boss thinking to herself, What else didn't he tell me? Does he always wait until the last minute? How often is he going to surprise me?

You have a disability and it is related to the job. You follow the teacher's instructions and after you are offered the job you say, "Oh, by the way. I have this disability which means I will need this 'reasonable accommodation'." Well, the employer doesn't agree with your definition of "reasonable" and, moreover, she does not like the fact that you waited until the last minute to tell her. (In fact, you literally wait until the *first* minute to tell her!) It looks like you are preparing for a lawsuit, not a new job! So she rescinds the offer not because of the "accommodation" issue but, more importantly, because she does not trust you. What else are you hiding? Employers do not like to be surprised.

Remember what I wrote earlier about veterans and the 800-pound gorilla, being up-front and honest? It applies to anyone who has to request a "reasonable accommodation" from an employer. How do I know I am right? Because it has worked for me personally, and for my career counseling clients.

Follow up. Now we come to the deal maker or the deal breaker. Do well, you have a chance. Do poorly...

At the end of the interview you thanked that interviewers and told them that you were very much interested in the position. You asked what the next step was. They told you that they would be in touch with no time indicated, in two weeks, or that you should call them in two weeks. You thanked them and you left.

That day, no excuses being acceptable, you sent a *personalized* thank-you email to *each* of the individuals who interviewed you. *Personalized* is the key word. Each has to be different. While, basically, they will all begin and end pretty much the same, it is the middle of the email that is important.

A good thank-you email can resurrect a bad interview. A bad thank-you email can destroy a good interview.

However you address the interviewer(s) in the interview(s), that is how you address them in the email:

> *Kathy,*
>
> *Thank you so much for having met with me today to discuss the director of Marketing position. I greatly appreciate your time and candor.*
>
> *I will not even try to express how much I desire to join your team and be a part of XYZ Inc.'s future.*
>
> *Thank you again for considering me. I look forward to hearing from.*
>
> *Sincerely,*
> *An Idiot Who Will Not Be Getting a Job Offer*

Too harsh? No. That email could have been sent to anyone for any job, from dog catcher to president. It is totally meaningless and totally worthless. I told you, it has to be *personalized*.

The purpose of the thank-you is to show that you immediately follow-up with people with whom you meet and that you can write professionally. It affords you an opportunity to confirm what is important, to correct any error(s) you made, and to clarify anything that needs clarification. But, most importantly, it is your one and only opportunity to show your interviewer(s) that you listened to what they said, you understood them, and you are on-board.

So how do you personalize the thank-you letter? Focus on the answer to the, "If I were to get this job, how would I be able to make your life easier?" question; or on the first unique question that each interviewer asked you (the assumption being that that is the issue most important to them); or, if a passionate discussion occurred during a group interview, focus on that topic for the individual who made it a passionate discussion. It is a judgment call; the choice is yours.

It should go something like this:

> *Kathy,*
>
> *Thank you for meeting with me today to discuss the director of Marketing position.*
>
> *If I may, I just want to clarify something I said so there is no misunderstanding. I believe I misspoke when I told you that the campaign for our new widget resulted in our having to hire 25 new manufacturing employees. It was, in fact, 35.*
>
> *I greatly appreciate your candor in telling me that you need someone who will work closely with Sales. As you know, I have a great deal of experience navigating the sensitive relationship between Sales and Marketing. I have successfully done it for others; I can and will do it for you.*
>
> *Thanks again. I look forward to hearing from you.*
>
> *Sincerely,*
> *A Good Candidate Who May Just Get The Job*

See the difference? Now it has substance. This candidate made an honest mistake and corrected it. Nothing wrong with that; it's called being human. But they also told the recipient that they were listening and can solve the specific problem that that person had raised during the interview.

Again, that email goes out on the day of the interview. Period. No excuses. And please, proofread it before you hit "Send." Typos can cost job offers!

What you can send the next day is a handwritten note to the lead person who interviewed you. Unlike the email, this note need not go to everyone. Keep it short and simple.

> *Kathy,*
>
> *I just wanted to thank you again for interviewing me yesterday for the Marketing position. Rest assured that I am enthusiastic about joining your team and am confident that I can properly address the issues we discussed. Needless to say, I hope to hear from you soon.*
>
> *Best,*
> *Good Candidate*

If you have lousy handwriting, not to worry, just print. It is the thought that counts!

Kathy told you she would be in touch sometime in the future. You have not heard from her. She told you she would call in two weeks. She hasn't. Kathy told you to call her in two weeks. You did. She didn't take the call so you left a message on her voice mail. She never got back to you. Happy, you are not.

What do you do? First, things happen. There was an emergency. God forbid, someone died. It could be any number of things that throws a hiring schedule off. So give it another week and, if you still don't hear from her, send a "Thank-You Rejection Letter." (If they did not give you a timeline, wait a month and then send the letter.) It goes like this, and, you can also send it if you are formally rejected, which does not always happen because employers are worried about being sued for discrimination, not to mention the fact they do not like unpleasant phone calls. This is ironic because, when I call candidates to tell them that they have been rejected, only rarely do they respond unprofessionally. Most are grateful for the call, the follow up. Here's the letter:

Interviewing

Kathy,

Thank you again for having interviewed me for the director of Marketing position. While I am naturally disappointed that I have not been made an offer, I appreciate the opportunity and wish you and your new hire the very best.

I look forward to our paths crossing once again.

Sincerely,
A Classy Rejected Candidate

When I wrote about this on LinkedIn I was surprised by the number of people who responded that they had sent similar letters and had, like the couple of cases I had previously heard about, received job offers from the companies that had rejected them, albeit not for the original positions for which they had applied. Because of the letter – and it is a letter: Paper, envelope, stamp, old-school – they were remembered.

If, when the letter arrives, it turns out that you have not been rejected, that's perfectly alright. Unlike other candidates who may have called or ignored the silence, you responded in a professional manner. You showed that you have great customer service skills and that you are a class act.

And if you were correct, and you were rejected, again, you acted in a professional manner. You showed that you have great customer service skills and you are a class act.

Truth be told, you will be rejected by most employers. As I wrote earlier, a job search is a numbers game. Only one person is going to get the job. Usually, there are between three and five finalists. Calculate your odds.

No one likes rejection and, when it comes to a job search, it is only natural to take it personally. And that can lead to depression. Many people just want to give up. But it isn't personal; it's a business decision. They decided that, for the good of the company, another candidate was more suited for the position. Your turn will come.

Human nature being what it is, since everyone is a minority in one way or another, we immediately think we are being discriminated against. Well, we aren't. We might be, but the odds are so slim it is not worth obsessing over. But it is an important subject. While I have already touched upon it, I want to delve deeper.

Discrimination

I'm sorry, but this entire section reminds me of the child who comes home from school, having failed a test, crying, "The teacher hates me!" It could happen, but it could also be the fact that when asked (and as I understand it this really happened), "Where did they sign the Declaration of Independence?" the student responded, "On the bottom of the page!"

You didn't get the job. You're African-American, Hispanic, Asian. You can't hide it. It is very noticeable. They are going to figure it out the minute you walk in the door. Maybe they looked at your Profile photo on LinkedIn and knew you were a...whatever. So they went to all the trouble to bring you in for an interview so that you could be one of the token...whatevers...that they interviewed to be able to prove that they do not discriminate?

Well, you can't do anything about your race so there was nothing you could have done to prevent the discrimination. And, of course, it's almost impossible to prove discrimination and, no doubt, very costly. So you did not get the job and now you are crying about not being able to work for a bigot and help her grow her business?!

You didn't get the job. You are religious. You walked in with your head covered and/or wearing a religious symbol around your neck. Well, you could have hid it but, if you need a "reasonable accommodation" because of your religious beliefs, that would not have been a wise move. As discussed, maybe what you consider "reasonable" the employer would not. And maybe the employer would be right. So you were wise not to hide your religion. And if you did not get the job because the job would require you to work on the Sabbath, sorry, but that's not discrimination. You are not qualified to do the job because you cannot fulfill the requirements. If you did not get the job because of your religious beliefs, *that's* discrimination and for all intents and purposes, you will never be able to prove it.

You didn't get the job. You are old. At least you consider yourself old. So you were discriminated against. Reread everything you just read. But in this case, there is a difference. Yes, there are plenty of ways to overcome old age, so to speak, and to turn age into an advantage over those young whippersnappers. You didn't know how so you didn't do it and the interviewers did not want to hire their Gramps or Granny. You blew it! Sorry, this one is on you.

Alright, since you are asking, I will remind you what you should have done. Focus on the fact that you have a wealth of experience dealing with adversity. You don't panic. You can calmly, and rationally, resolve the matter. Also mention that you are looking for a long-term commitment. And highlight the fact that throughout your career you have had to learn and adapt to change. You are not stuck in your ways. Make it clear that you are not looking to take over your supervisor's job, the person who is interviewing you! Your "Big Bird Story" should be about how you have been a mentor to colleagues and helped them advance in their careers. To emphasize that, note that one of your references will be a former colleague who you mentored and who went on to bigger and better. Finally, make sure you do not look old. Good posture and a firm handshake will help. Age should never be a problem in anyone's mind. Ironically, if it is in yours, it will be in others!

My attitude is to believe that the reason you probably did not get the job is because there was a better candidate. It has nothing to do with your race, religion, age, or whatever. That should also be your attitude. Why?

There are some things you can do nothing about. What do they say? "Don't worry about the things you can't change, worry about the things you can." You can't turn a bigot, a racist, a sexist or any other "ist" into a decent human being. It is not going to happen. But you can turn yourself into a better candidate.

I know this is emotional, but I also know I am right. I had one man come to me convinced that he needed a new résumé because he was not getting any interviews. He was certain it was because of discrimination. Yes, he needed a new résumé. But I made him read the résumé out loud. I then asked him, "What in the résumé reveals that you are an X?" He had to admit that there was nothing. It was a bad résumé and that was why the phone was not ringing.

My message to you is this: Consider the possibility that you may need to improve. If all you are going to do is whine and cry "Discrimination!" you will not learn from the experience and, as they say, "If you keep on doing what you have always done, you will keep on getting what you have always gotten." Or, if you prefer

Einstein, "The definition of insanity is doing the same thing and expecting different results."

Don't whine; be open to the possibility that you are doing something wrong. Find out what it is, and fix it. Then you should start getting interview and offers. Play the victim, and get used to watching afternoon television.

But just as with interviewing, I shall not end on a negative, but rather a positive. Congratulations! You got the job offer. Now you have to negotiate.

Part Four: Negotiating

Negotiating is the art of compromise when the parties are equals. A candidate and an employer may be equals, but only if the employer really wants the candidate and can't find anyone else, and the candidate really needs the job – which reminds me, never come across as desperate. No one hires people out of sympathy.

Of course, with employment, there may be no negotiations. It can be "take it or leave it." The parties are not equal. It happens all the time. And then you have to make a decision. If an employer ever insists on an immediate response, reject the offer. Something is very wrong and you don't want to find out what it is.

Because I am not an attorney, I am not going to discuss employment contracts and how to negotiate, most importantly, severance. The majority of us will never have the proverbial "golden parachute." What we, the common folk, receive is an "Offer Letter." But before they make the offer, in all likelihood they will, hopefully, check your references and then, if all goes well, ask your permission to conduct a background check.

References. Most people think that references are a waste of time. (For the record, "Letters of Reference" are! A reference with whom a recruiter or employer cannot speak is not a reference.) Who is going to give the name of someone who will give them a negative reference? Based on my experience, plenty of people. It is surprising what references will say when made to feel comfortable.

In any event, usually three professional references will suffice. Ideally, they should be former supervisors. Only rarely will a reference from a current employer be needed. If supervisors are not available, peers, board members, even vendors, may suffice, but you will have to explain why you can't provide a supervisor as a reference.

Do not give an employer the names and contact information of your references until you have spoken with them. First, you need to confirm that they will provide the reference. Second, you need to confirm that they are available. There is nothing worse than calling a reference, leaving a message, and never hearing from them. The immediate conclusion is, they don't like the person! Third, you need to prep them. You have to make certain that they will mention the correct things. They have to reinforce what you said in the interview(s), not add items to the discussion.

107

If all goes well with the references, you may receive a conditional offer letter stating that they will formally offer you the position, conditional upon the results of the background check.

Background Check. For many positions, especially positions where you will be dealing with money or in healthcare, a background check will be required. You will have to give permission in writing. As already stated, this is the time you provide your Social Security Number.

Usually, they will check for criminal convictions and your driving record. In some jurisdictions they are permitted to conduct a credit check. Regardless, you know what negatives they may discover. Tell them up front. They will respect you and appreciate it. Employers, especially as the hiring process is concluding, do not like surprises. Explain things to them and, usually, not always, but usually, the issue will never become an issue.

Additionally, you may be required to take a drug test and medical exam. All I can advise is don't eat poppy-seed bagels! (No, it didn't happen to me but a friend's urine test came back positive for opiates.)

For our purposes, everything goes find. Now you receive the offer.

The Offer Letter

The Offer Letter is exactly what it sounds like. The employer offers you the job, usually confirming the title you will have and your salary. Benefits are standard and there may be no room for negotiations. Some companies have strict salary limits and no flexibility when it comes to benefits. But sometimes there is some flexibility regarding, at least, salary. But don't forget, benefits are money too! This is especially true regarding pension; life, short- and long-term disability, and health insurance.

Most times, all things being equal, an employer will offer a candidate anywhere from 10 to 15% above their current salary, to make the move worthwhile. (It may be more if the person has to relocate and the offer will usually include moving expenses.) This is reasonable. If the new job will include significant new responsibilities, the offer should be higher. Everything should be stipulated in the letter. The last thing you want is misunderstandings when it comes to your compensation package.

Negotiating

An aside, if I may, for veterans. Your pay was not like a civilian's. Part of your pay was housing, clothes, and food. So, when negotiating you quote your salary saying "not including benefits," make certain the employer understands what your benefits were, if you did not discuss it during the interview(s). And for everyone, never raise the issue of salary during an interview. It is for the employer to raise.

Whatever you told the employer were your salary expectations, are only the basis of the negotiations. Unless they actually offer what you asked for, you can always make one counter proposal. And even if they do meet your number, you can try to get more by claiming not to have understood the complexity of the position prior to the interview(s), and also bring up the fact that your present benefits, if it is true, are better than what they are offering.

If the offer is too low, show them the budget you prepared. Tell them what you need and ask them to match it. If they refuse, suggest that they meet you half way now and, in six months, consider giving you the difference. Sometimes, this works. In any event, this is not a long, drawn out negotiation. If you don't reach an agreement quickly, they will move on.

Usually there will be a probationary period. Do not worry about it. If you live in a state like New York, where all non-contracted employees are "at-will," you can be fired at any time. So don't give it too much thought.

As stated, never make an immediate decision. Ask how much time you have and never accept less than one day. I had two candidates, for two different executive recruiting clients, both of whom were offered $10,000 increases. They went home, discussed the offers with their wives, and rejected them. Their wives said, "No." And they were right!

The first explained to me that the new job would involve a commute. It meant paying daily tolls and wear-and-tear on the family car. He prepared an Excel spreadsheet showing that for tolls and gas alone, he would be paying $5,000. I spoke to the client and they immediately agreed to raise their offer by $5,000.

As for the second, the new employer's health insurance was going to cost him $5,000 more than what he was currently paying. Again, the client raised the offer by $5,000.

It is really very simple: You don't lose out on a good candidate, and start the process all over again, for a measly five grand.

Do not under any circumstances resign until you have an offer letter in hand. Paper or email, does not matter. It is not real until you have it in writing. At that point, resign.

Resigning

You never want to burn bridges. The normal practice is to offer your resignation effective your length of vacation. If you have two-weeks vacation, you give two-weeks notice. No rational employer will object to your giving notice. After all, if you walk out on your current employer today, you may walk out on *them* tomorrow.

Put the resignation in writing, and praise your supervisor(s) and colleagues. Mention a few successes you had of which you are particularly proud. Why? Because if someone decides to put something negative in your file, you want to make certain there is balance. But the truth is, it does not matter. What are the odds that anyone will ever look at it?

Leave on the best of terms. Make certain your colleagues know where everything is in your office. Explain your filing system, what you are working on, and what needs to be done. Be available to take calls if they have any questions. You may still need these people, especially your supervisor, because, in a number of years, you may be asking them for a reference!

One thing: *Never* accept a counteroffer. Your reputation will be hurt. The new employer will be furious. And life at work will not be pleasant. Your colleagues will resent the fact that you got a raise for being disloyal. People may resign if *they* don't get raises. After all, they were loyal; you weren't. And the bosses will not trust you. There is never a good reason to accept a counteroffer. Period. End of sentence. End of Discussion. And, come to think of it, end of book.

About the Author

Bruce A. Hurwitz, Ph.D., president of Hurwitz Strategic Staffing, Ltd., whose mission it is to promote the hiring of veterans, has been an executive recruiter since 2003 and a career counselor since 2009. He is a recognized authority on career counseling, recruitment, and employment issues, having been cited in over 700 articles, appearing in some 500 publications, across the United States, and in at least 30 foreign countries. His posts on LinkedIn have been read some 400,000 times and have garnered national and international media attention, including appearances on the Fox Business Network, Headline News (CNN), the local New York Fox affiliate, and a mention on ABC's *Good Morning America*. A "Five-Star" speech writer on Fiverr, he is also the host of the live business interview podcast, *Bruce Hurwitz Presents*.

Prior to becoming a recruiter, he was a non-profit professional. An honors graduate of the Hebrew University of Jerusalem, Israel, where he earned his Ph.D. in International Relations, he has over 125 peer-reviewed books, articles and newspaper contributions, on topics ranging from International Relations and International Law to the use of technology to conducting an effective job search to having a successful career.

===

If you have found this book of help, and would like personal assistance, please visit the Career Counseling page on Bruce Hurwitz's website, www.hsstaffing.com, to engage his services.